Linda Dannenberg

# NEW
FRENCH
COUNTRY
A Style and Source Book

Photographs by Guy Bouchet

Clarkson Potter/Publishers
New York

Copyright © 2004
by Linda Dannenberg
Photographs copyright © 2004
by Guy Bouchet

Published by Clarkson Potter/Publishers, New York. Member of the Crown Publishing Group, a division of Random House, Inc. www.crownpublishing.com

CLARKSON N. POTTER is a trademark and POTTER and colophon are registered trademarks of Random House, Inc.

Printed in China

Design by Julio Vega

Endpaper fabric design "Vertoui" courtesy of Les Olivades

Library of Congress Cataloging-in-Publication Data
Dannenberg, Linda.
New French country: a style and source book / Linda Dannenberg; photographs by Guy Bouchet.
1. Decoration and ornament, Rustic—France—Provence.
2. Provence (France)—Social life and customs. I. Title.
NK1449.A3.D36 2004
745.4'49449—dc21 2003009186

ISBN 0-609-61041-4

10 9 8 7 6 5 4

First Edition

PAGE ONE *A restored mas (farmhouse) in Saint-Étienne du Grès.* PRECEDING PAGES *A gathering of Arlésienne santons adorns an 18th-century mantel at the Hôtel du Castellet; they were designed by Nono Girard and produced by Arterra in Marseille.* OVERLEAF *A romantic garden in the Alpilles was inspired by Florence's Boboli Gardens.*

ACKNOWLEDGMENTS

New French Country reflects a unique world of friendship and generosity. The help and enthusiastic involvement of many people—those who opened their doors to us, those who facilitated the opening of other doors, and those who offered suggestions that led to countless wonderful discoveries—made this book possible. To all of these people, friends, colleagues, and acquaintances old and new, our sincere appreciation and gratitude: Laurence and David Ambrose; Nancy Antik; Roseline Bacou; Ghyslaine Beguin; René, Danièle, and Sandra Bérard; Mireille Blanc; Vincent Boeuf; Lucille and Jacques Bon; Gaspard Borgeaud; Olivier Borloo; Hugues Bosc; Françoise and Jean-Pierre Boudin-Conte; Jean-Jacques Bourgeois; Chantal Bresson-Tissot; Marie-Claude Brochet; André Cabanel; Serge Cagnolari; Nicole Cappeau; Bruno Carles; André Chabert; Marie-Pierre Champagne; Jean-André and Geneviève Charial; Dominique Cornwell; Agnès Costa; Frédéric Dervieux; Alain Ducasse; Marie-Catherine Dupuy; Philippe Eckert; Florence Costa Fabre; Pierre Faucon; Elisabeth Ferriol; Marion Fourestier of the Maison de la France; Joël Fournier; Nono Girard; Philippe Gurdjian; Dominique and Etienne Hardy; Bibi and Guy Hervais; Rosann Valentini Katan; Daniel Kiener; Annie and Henri Laurent; Catherine Ligeard; Marco Lillet; Daniela McLean; Florence Maeght; Jean-Pierre Margan; Robin Massee of the Maison de la France; Caroline Maurin; Edith Mézard; Patrice Mullin-Jones; Francine Nicolle; Hannelore and Renato de Paolis; Antony Pitot; Estelle Réale; Robert Reyre; Caroline Rostang; Michel Rostang; Michel Semini; Vicki de Serveras; Nathalie Savalli; Jocelyne Sibuet; Martin Stein; Hervé Thibault; Madame Vadon; Gertjan van der Hoest; Mr. and Mrs. Armand Ventilo; Brigitte Benoît-Vernin; and Stanley and Lorenzo Weisman.

Special thanks go to Kathy and Lloyd Otterman, in the Luberon, and to Marie-Colette and Jean-Michel Borgeaud in Fontvieille, for their friendship and their warm welcomes during my many visits to Provence. The happy, memorable times spent in their homes and at their tables enriched the many months spent creating this book.

I want to express my deep appreciation to Hélène Lafforgue, a woman of great taste, style, and talent, whose contacts and expertise opened many doors.

I am, as I have been for so many years, extremely grateful to my wonderful agent, Gayle Benderoff, whose wise counsel and constant support smoothes every book's passage from conception to publication, and whose warm friendship enhances the pleasure of every new project.

To all my friends and colleagues at Clarkson Potter, whose hard work, talent, and extraordinary editorial skills were crucial to the creation of this book, I express my heartfelt appreciation: Lauren Shakely, an insightful publisher and friend who was so helpful and enthusiastic when the idea for this book was first broached; fine editors Rosy Ngo and Roy Finamore; Jennifer Defilippi; Barbara Marks; Jane Treuhaft; Mark McCauslin; Joan Denman; and to Julio Vega for his inspired design that captures the distinct charm, personality, and joie de vivre of the French countryside.

Lastly, warmest and most affectionate thanks to my husband, Steve, and my son, Ben, for their understanding of the time and travel this book required, and for their constant love and support.

To the memory of Pierre Moulin & Pierre LeVec
⟨En souvenir de leur amitié et de leur joie de vivre

CONTENTS

INTRODUCTION

A little more than twenty years ago, I arrived in Provence with the late Pierre Moulin and Pierre Le Vec, founders of Pierre Deux, the widely influential group of French Country antiques and decoration shops. This endearing and dynamic duo, more than anyone or anything else, was responsible for introducing the concept of French Country style to the United States. Our mission during this long-ago summer was to create a book on the style and lifestyle of the south of France. After several weeks of research and scouting, photographer Guy Bouchet came to join us, and the book that eventually became *Pierre Deux's French Country* was on its way. "French Country" as a name and an articulated style was in its infancy back then. But over the past two decades, "French Country" grew from a mode of furnishing into a craze and eventually into a global lifestyle phenomenon. "French Country" these days is as much about image as it is about style. The phrase conjures not just thoughts of a fine walnut armoire and brightly printed

cotton curtains, but visions of endless, sunny days, sitting on the terrace of a village café sipping chilled rosé; of climbing the rugged hills of the Luberon up to a rustic country auberge for its savory Sunday lunches; of listening to Verdi's *La Traviata* under the stars in Aix-en-Provence; of hunting for the perfect 18th-century buffet or 19th-century limestone mantel in the antiques shops of L'Isle-sur-la-Sorgue; and of visiting the Abbaye de Sénanque, surrounded by vast lavender gardens, and—whatever your religious persuasion—attending the remarkable mass of Gregorian chants early on a Sunday morning.

Beyond happy dreams of being there, French Country now is also about bringing the best of what's there home, tapping into the finest and most authentic elements and ideas that the rural regions of France—especially the south of France—have to offer and adapting them to your environment, wherever in the world that may be. The mistral may not howl down your chimney, and the sun may not be a powerful, shimmering aura outside your window, but the fabrics, the furniture, the crafts, and the cuisine will be within, and with them the exuberant spirit and charm of the French countryside.

PRECEDING PAGES On the Plateau de Valensole in the Alpes-de-Haute-Provence, fields of commercially planted lavender cultivated in long neat rows await the mid-summer harvest. RIGHT *From the fine collection of vintage posters at the Mas des Fontaines, a turn-of-the-century poster by David Delleprat touts the bucolic pleasures of Provence.* OPPOSITE *Sunset tints the hill town of Bonnieux with a rosy glow.*

Almost twenty-five years on, French Country style is as popular as ever, if not more so, thanks not only to the long-lived international success of *Pierre Deux's French Country,* which amazed and humbled us, but also to other, later books such as Peter Mayle's *A Year in Provence* and *Toujours Provence,* which fueled fresh dreams of this region. Disseminating the style to a vast new audience were the scores of decorators and decorating catalogues that picked up and perpetuated the French Country theme. Over the past two decades, I have revisited Provence many times for both work and vacations, and I noted each time how Provence was evolving. Old fabric companies were modernized if not reinvented, producing high-quality fabrics in captivating new patterns or newly adapted antique patterns, the textiles growing beyond the classic floral-sprigged cottons to sophisticated toiles, subtle stripes, and handsome jacquard weaves. Superb restorations of antique houses in a wide variety of styles were proliferating from the mountains to the sea. Enchanting new hotels and bed-and-breakfast inns were springing up. Gardens were blooming where before they had gone to seed, or not existed at all. And, distinctly noticeable, the decorative palette of Provence was growing more varied and sophisticated, expanding from the bright signature hues of russet, ocher, sunflower, vivid green, and rich blue to more subtle beige, grège, sand, mauve, and pale olive. The old artisans—most of them, anyway—were still there, but there were new artisans as well, inspired by the old traditions while bringing a fresh contemporary vision to their work. Authentic regional antiques were becoming progressively harder to find. The rare, majestically proportioned 18th-century architect's desk offered for $15,000 in 1982 couldn't be found for three times the price today; ditto for the gorgeous 18th-century lavishly carved *buffet-à–glissants* I saw in Le Paradou for $10,000 and have been dreaming about ever since, *hélas.* But the best antiques dealers had begun to produce beautifully handcrafted reproductions, which were displayed with pride in many of the finest houses I visited, right alongside the classic antiques.

With the Midi more alluring than ever, I believed it was time to go back and reexamine French Country style in Provence, to research the

PRECEDING PAGES, LEFT *Beneath a Russian still life bought at an auction in Paris, an early-20th-century butcher's table holds appetizers for an alfresco dinner.* PRECEDING PAGES, RIGHT *At the lively Saturday-morning market on the Place Richelme in Aix-en-Provence, local nuns sell produce from their abbey's farm.* OPPOSITE *On the shaded terrace of a home near Lacoste, an antique* terre mélée *(mixed-earth) bowl from Apt holds gourds, their color mirroring several of the shades in the bowl's tinted clays.*

best of what was old, and had continued on, and what was new with incipient staying power; in short, to present a *new* French Country to all those who love the style, the region, and everything it represents, as I do. Over the course of two years, I had the opportunity and pleasure to spend many months in Provence, traveling everywhere from the tip of the Drôme, just below Valence, south to the Mediterranean, and from west of the Rhône east to the Italian border. This book has been a remarkable and privileged journey.

The Provence of today is a bit more developed in some areas; less rural, less "undiscovered" in many areas; more expensive everywhere; and yet, still the Provence of our dreams. The land is rich, diverse, and uniquely luminous, characteristics reflected in every style domain: fur- niture, architecture, tiles, fabrics, crafts, and gardens. A fertile, sun- baked region of southern France, Provence has a charm so distinctive, traditions so deeply rooted, and a joie de vivre so contagious that it truly stands alone.

Regional style in every French province, while not unaffected by the prevailing trends in Paris, is always more a product of the land and its people than it is of the mode of the capital and the court. It is deter- mined by practical rather than fashionable considerations: lifestyle, cli- mate, geography, and available materials. But in Provence, beyond these

PRECEDING PAGES *A leafy canopy formed by plane trees shelters a private lane in Fortvielle.* ABOVE LEFT *Provence by the sea: a fishing boat cruises along the* calanques *(chalky cliffs) that rise from the coast west of Marseille.* RIGHT *An enfilade of narrow houses overlooks the harbor in Martigues.* BELOW *At the end of the day, fishing boats crowd back in the harbor of Marseille's Vieux Port.* OPPOSITE *In the cozy harbor of Port du Niel, near Toulon, small fishing boats called* pointus—*for their distinctive pointed-at-both-ends design—moor in the Mediterranean's deliciously clear and inviting water.*

basic elements, there were also a number of outside influences that made their mark on what became *le style provençal.* Enhancing the landscape, particularly in southwestern Provence, was and is the very visible heritage from the Phoenicians and the Romans, master builders with a great sense of proportion and style who left their mark on the land from their thriving civilizations before and just after the birth of Christ. Many rustic farmhouses today were built with ancient Roman stones found lying partially buried in fields. Later, in the 17th and 18th centuries, came craftsmen from Italy—painters, sculptors, tile workers—traveling north to look for work; master *ferronniers*—artisans in wrought and cast iron—from Spain; and the East India merchant ships that sailed into and out of the port of Marseille, unloading their exotic and colorful Oriental cargoes on the Provençal shores. But the influences on Provence were gentle. They served, for the most part, to expand rather than to transform the vision of the Provençal artists and artisans.

French Country is not one style but many. Tucked into the hills and dotting the plains are small, simple farmhouses; vast estates with park-like gardens; and sun-bleached ranches. Tiny, cleverly designed pieds-à-terre are ensconced behind antique walls of beautiful old cities such as Avignon. The style of the French countryside has evolved over hundreds of years, arriving at a look that is appealingly genuine and perfectly adapted to its time and place. It is not a conceit imposed by a sovereign—although Louis XV and Louis XVI certainly had a bit of trickle-down influence—or a particular school of design. Inside the cottages, châteaux, and farmhouses of Provence there is little effort to make everything match, or even to maintain a continuity of periods. The French mix what they like with what they need with what the family has handed down. The look is eclectic and yet cohesive.

ABOVE Tauromachie *(anything relating to bulls and bullfighting) is a frequent decorative theme throughout Provence. Some homes are adorned with the heads or skulls of actual bulls, but chez Marco Lillet in Eygalières, a simple bull's head woven from young grapevines presides over the terrace.* OPPOSITE *A group of* gardiens *(the horsemen of the Camargue) prepares to parade around an arena before a bullfight in Mouriès. Mounted on distinctive white Camarguais horses, and garbed in their traditional velour dress jackets, the* gardiens *are an integral part of the village's annual September* Fête aux Olives Vertes *(The Green Olive Festival), a daylong affair of markets, parades, bullfights, and free-flowing wine.*

French Country style can be interpreted and exemplified in many different ways. Still, there are some basic markers and characteristics to guide you. In general, it is more rustic than refined, although refinement is certainly not absent in the French Country look. The style was aptly described once by *Women's Wear Daily,* in writing about several houses in Saint-Rémy-de-Provence, as *"chic rustique."* French Country glassware, for example, is chunky, hand-blown bubbled glass, rather than faceted lead crystal. Fabrics are beige linen, vegetable-dyed muslins, vibrantly printed cottons in 18th-century-inspired paisleys, or lushly textured toiles rather than pastel silk damasks and fussy brocades. Tableware is not the fine bone china of Sèvres, but the red-clay faience of Moustiers, Apt, and Aubagne. Furniture is rush-seated, such as on the armchairs of Vallabrègues, rather than upholstered. *Chic rustique* extends even to the rooftops of Provençal homes, which disdain the sleek symmetry of a slate-roofed Paris town house or a Loire Valley château in favor of a mosaic of undulating mottled canal tiles that form roofs tipped at odd angles.

Never stylized, never contrived, and never pretentious, *le style provençal* in all of its manifestations is distinctive, comfortable, appealing, and exquisitely crafted. The massive 18th-century walnut armoires carved by local craftsmen in Arles or Fourques will last a millennium; the sensuous, sculpted stone mantelpieces from Les Baux will endure even longer.

To find myself back in Provence, in a little cottage near Les Baux-de-Provence set between olive groves and a field of poppies, was my own Proust-like experience of finding *le temps perdu.* Sitting in the garden on a string of balmy evenings, watching the sun set through the silvery leaves of the olive trees, I was, as I had been during my very first sojourn in Provence, overwhelmed by the countryside's intoxicating effect on the senses. The air here is heady with the powerful, aromatic fragrances of rosemary, thyme, and lavender; the winds, from the gentle breezes to the relentless mistral, cool the brow and cleanse the air; and, at nightfall, the chirping of the cicadas—*les cigales*—rings long after the actual song is over. This is the immutable Provence I love.

THE COLORS OF THE COUNTRY

The color here is really very beautiful," Vincent van Gogh wrote in a letter from Arles to his brother Theo. "When the green is fresh it is a rich green like we rarely see in the north, a soothing green. When it is burnished, covered with dust, it does not become ugly for it, but the countryside then takes on gilded tones in all the nuances: green gold, yellow gold, pink gold, or bronzed, or coppery, and from lemon gold to an umber yellow, the yellow for example of a heap of

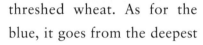

PRECEDING PAGES At the Mas de la Barjolle, an olive-oil producing estate in Fontvieille, a regiment of baby olive trees stands at attention in a field of poppies; plastic cones protect the little plants from rabbits. ABOVE LEFT *The natural affinity between yellows and greens is apparent in the pairing of these hues throughout Provence. Usually yellow is dominant, while green is the accent color. Two shades of green, on the grapevine's leaves and the painted shutter, accent the yellow wall of a house near Mouriès.* ABOVE RIGHT *The celadon hue of a bedroom door softly contrasts with creamy yellow walls in the hallway of a home in Villeneuve-lès-Avignon.* OPPOSITE *Showing their age but soldiering on, a deep green 18th-century* cruche de barque *(ship's water jug) and a 19th-century vegetable-dyed piqué quilt keep company in the private collection of a farmer near Nîmes.*

threshed wheat. As for the blue, it goes from the deepest royal blue in the water to the blue of forget-me-nots, to cobalt, especially to a pale, transparent blue, to blue-green to blue-violet."

The warm, rich, intense colors of Provence are dazzling, particularly so on a day when the air is swept to crystalline clarity by the mistral. The characteristic ochers, russets, silver-green, cerulean blues, deep roses, alizarin reds, sunflower yellow, and variegated lavenders of the Provençal canvas are the colors of the earth, the flowers, and the sky. Intrinsic components of the French Country look, the colors of the landscape have been picked up and adapted in fabrics, tiles, furniture, and interior and exterior décor.

In the lavish Provençal palette, a palette that inspired Matisse, Van Gogh, Cézanne, Chagall, and countless other artists, each color is in reality not a single color but a variety of subtle hues, which change according to the light. In earliest morning, the colors have a soft, silvery cast. At high noon, they are bleached flat by the white-ringed sun. In the slanting rays of late afternoon, the colors are burnished, deepening and intensifying to almost over-lush saturation. Finally, just after sunset, the world is washed in soft lavender before graying into the night.

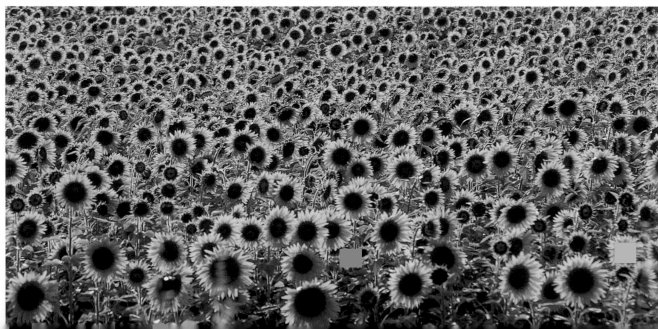

LES JAUNES

LEFT *The luminous bathroom of a 17th-century farmhouse sports flax-hued walls accented by a green-bordered* oeil-de-boeuf *(bull's-eye) window.* RIGHT *Ocher-yellow tiles alternate with brown and white in a guest bathroom at the Clos des Saumanes, a bed-and-breakfast near Avignon.* BELOW *At the Mas de Peint, a hotel in the Camargue, black-and-white checked curtains and a cozy late-19th-century loveseat enhance the buff-yellow salon.* OPPOSITE, CLOCKWISE FROM TOP LEFT *A golden ocher hue enlivens the facade of a bastide near Grasse; the brilliant blossoms of the mimosa bush are a happy sign of spring; the elegant yellow walls of the Fragonard museum form a backdrop to a collection of romantic early-18th-century paintings, this one by Coypel; sunflowers turn their heads to the sun outside of Saint-Rémy; in the guest bedroom of a home in Eygalières, antique prints show to advantage against the pale saffron walls.*

Perhaps the most defining colors of Provence are the **ochers, russets,** and earthy **pinks,** the colors that spring from the earth in the Luberon. In the captivating hill town of Roussillon, distinguished by its pink- and gold-hued houses, and beyond in the towns of Rustrel and Gargas, near Apt, the earth itself is red or yellow-gold, dense with iron-rich pink or ocher ore. This bounty of ocher was discovered and exploited already in the time of the Romans; the ore could be quarried and processed to yield powdered ocher pigments. By the 1800s, many in the region made their livings mining, extracting, washing, sifting, and crushing the sandy ore for pigment. The traditional and distinctive colors from the pigments became part of the region's vernacular style, distinguishing fabrics, tiles, faience, occasionally furniture, as well as houses. Enriching the pink-yellow portion of the palette is the glowing, golden limestone. The color of wheat in the afternoon sun, the limestone is quarried in the Vaucluse and the Bouches-du-Rhône and is used to build the sturdy farmhouses and grand *bastides* (country estates) throughout Provence. Further on in the yellow spectrum is a frank, bright yellow, which also stems from the earth, although not as a mineral. This is the yellow of

⌒OPPOSITE In the Ancienne Usine Mathieu's former storeroom, now part of the Conservatoire des Ocres museum, piles of raw, quarried ocher reveal the naturally vivid hues that eventually tint pigments and paints.⌒

COLOR AND LIGHT

A fascinating stop, if you happen to be visiting Roussillon, is the Ancienne Usine Mathieu/Conservatoire des Ocres, a former pigment mill. Today the conservatory is dedicated to teaching both amateurs and professionals the art of working with color. There's a museum, a library, and a wide choice of courses and workshops throughout the year. The conservatory documents how the area developed into a world capital for the production of masterfully mixed natural pigments. Locally, the pigments were mixed into pink- or yellow-hued plaster or lime washes and slathered over the facades of houses large and small. Eventually, in the mid- to late 20th century, these colors began to make their way indoors, decorating kitchens, bedrooms, dining rooms, and living rooms.

⌒ABOVE At the Conservatoire des Ocres, antique color swatches form an intriguing mosaic in one of the former pigment factory's workrooms.⌒

⚛LES ROUGES

⚛LEFT *The vivid rose facade of this* mas *(farmhouse) near Saint-Rémy gives new life to a classic old residence.* RIGHT *Light billows into a small russet bedroom at the Maison des Sources, a bed-and-breakfast in Lauris.* BELOW *In Roussillon, where many homes are washed with an ocher-red tint, a small third-floor window reflects a neighbor's canal-tile roof.* OPPOSITE, CLOCKWISE FROM TOP LEFT *A madder-red antique quilt makes a rich backdrop for an early-18th-century game platter from Saint-Jean de Fos; in Estelle Réale's charming guest house, the Villa Estelle, in Les Hauts-de-Cagnes, a delicate palette of pinks and terra-cottas enhances a stairway; two vintage gas pumps still stand sentinel in the Luberon village of Saint-Pantaléon; Orange's "The Four Winds" café adapts the colors of its neighbors in its Belle Epoque–style facade.*⚛

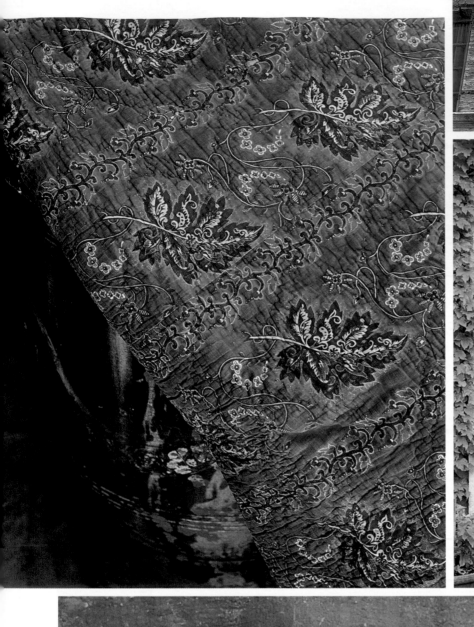

LES BLEUS

A mottled blue washes the bedroom walls of the Mas de la Beaume, a bed-and-breakfast in Gordes. RIGHT *An antique mailbox awaits the postman at the door of Vernin Carreaux d'Apt, a tile factory in Bonnieux.* BELOW *Time has weathered the once-rich blue of a village home's shutters, door, and trim in the Vaucluse.* OPPOSITE, CLOCKWISE FROM TOP LEFT *The varied blue tones of an early-19th-century quilt dyed with indigo have stood the test of time; hyacinth-blue accents the shutters of a limestone home near Les Baux de Provence; a blue that verges on turquoise embellishes a door in the countryside west of Nîmes; an antique wheelbarrow sports an old coat of pale blue, the Provençal farmer's traditional color of choice for wheelbarrows.*

LES MAUVES

LEFT *A luscious shade of mauve greets visitors at the doorway of the Villa Estelle in Les Hauts-de-Cagnes.* RIGHT *An old hardware and notions shop in the village of Sault, renowned for its lavender harvest, chose the flower's color to spiff up its vintage facade.* BELOW *A garden of lavender near Gordes reaches full bloom in mid-July.* OPPOSITE, CLOCKWISE FROM TOP LEFT *In May, a lavish cape of old wisteria drapes the facade of a house near Saint-Rémy; in the study of the Abbaye Saint-André in Villeneuve-lès-Avignon, a lavender-hued wall cabinet contrasts softly with butter-yellow walls; fresh violet figs are one of the succulent pleasures of summer in Provence; an elegant amethyst cloth drapes the long dining table at the Villa Estelle.*

huge sunflowers that turn their heads to follow the sun in the vast fields of the Alpilles.

The distinctive **blue**-painted wooden shutters, trim, and doors throughout Provence—and other provinces as well—have, at base, a very practical raison d'être. To prevent the wood from being destroyed by mildew or mites, the wood trim on houses was daubed with a wash that contained copper sulfate, the same blue-hued chemical compound that is sprayed on grapevines to prevent rot. Blue shutters against a pink or ocher facade long ago became a beloved signature of Provençal style. Today's high-tech paints and sealers preclude the need for copper sulfate to protect the wood, but the spectrum of lively blues lives on as the choice for architectural trim.

The hues of lavender blossoms can range from soft grayish blue to intensely purple. Fields with row upon row of gorgeous lavender, planted in precise parallel ranks, splash the countryside with vivid purple stripes or broad patchworks of lavender juxtaposed with wheat. The blooms last from May until the harvests in mid- to late summer. Boldly present in nature, the color **lavender** has been little used in interior or exterior decoration, until recently. Over the past couple of years, the color has made small inroads in newly minted, fashionable décors from Grasse to Saint-Rémy, along with another purple shade: grape. It still remains to be seen whether these two colors will have the decorative staying power of the region's more traditional pinks, yellows, blues, and greens.

The **green** of Provence is first and foremost olive green. Or more precisely, olive greens, since there are two distinct shades: the soft, silvered green of the olive leaves, and the richer, slightly yellowed green of the

OPPOSITE *A deep olive green enriches the walls of the dining room display at the Souleiado Museum in Tarascon, which shows to advantage a richly carved* commode provençale. ABOVE *the branches of a thriving olive tree shortly before the fall harvest is the best exemplar of the many olive hues.*

THE OLIVE HARVEST

Provence is often defined by its olive trees. There are some old *Provençaux* who declare that Provence begins and ends where the olive trees grow—from about 10 miles inland from the Mediterranean to just beyond Nyons in the north, high in the Drôme, and from Nice in the Alpes-Maritimes to the environs of Arles and the Rhône Delta. Whether or not you agree with this exacting definition, there's no denying that the olive is pervasive, as a symbol of peace and abundance in furniture and fabric, as a popular color in regional décor, and as an essential element in the region's agricultural economy, cuisine, and local crafts.

The Greeks brought olive trees to Provence more than 2,500 years ago, and the trees found a climate they loved, adapting beautifully in soil that was either sandy or chalky with limestone. Under the agricultural expertise of the Greeks, who cultivated and grafted the trees with great care, *les oliviers* rapidly became

ubiquitous throughout the region, renewing themselves generation after generation. Some magnificent old trees can reach almost 70 feet tall, but rarely are trees allowed to grow to that dimension nowadays. More than sixty varieties thrive here, with lovely names that roll off the tongue—*salonenque, verdule, bouteillan, picholine*—from the succulent black olives of Nyons to the tender green olives of Mouriès to the tiny deep purple olives of Nice. All olives start off green, but they ripen and darken the longer they stay on the vine. The early-eating olives are plucked

ABOVE Olive groves dot the landscape of the Alpilles region, stretching both east and west from Les Baux de Provence.
LEFT Enthusiastic twins, Gaspard and Robinson, gather olives during the November harvest at the Mas de la Barjolle in Fontvieille.

⌐ABOVE *Baguette toasts spread with tapenade, the delicious black-olive paste, are among the sunset appetizers at the home of chef Jean-André Charial.* ABOVE RIGHT *A carafe of extra-virgin olive oil just after pressing at the Mas de la Barjolle.* RIGHT *At the Fête aux Olives Vertes in Mouriès, market stalls feature baskets of the town's star product.*⌐

green in September, while the rich black olives are gathered late in November to be pressed for oil. The oils range from pale gold to amber to dark green, each with a personality, yet all with the ability to bring out the very best in other regional products, such as artichokes, tomatoes, peppers, eggplant, fennel, and zucchini, as well as the bounty from the local waters, red mullet, sea bass, and cod.

Les Olivades (the olive harvest), is a time of back-straining work followed by great joy, celebrated at the end by exuberant festivals throughout the region. One of the liveliest and most beautiful festivals celebrating the olive is the *Fête aux Olives Vertes* (the Green Olive Festival) in the village of Mouriès, not far from Les Baux. After a Sunday mass in the village church, local children bring a brimming basket of green olives to the altar, in a gesture of thanks for the abundance of the harvest. A long and splendid procession through the village follows, with families throughout the region, *bébés* to white-haired *grand-mères*, dressed in their finest traditional costumes. The women wear starched *coiffes* and long dresses, the men, velvet jackets, bright Provençal cotton shirts, and broad-brimmed black hats. Pulling fancifully decorated carriages and wagons are the magnificent white horses of the Camargue. After a long picnic lunch, the day ends at the ancient village arena where there's music, dancing, and a highly anticipated running of the local bulls. It's a day that leaves you with a noticeable afterglow, from the sun, the contagious high spirits and excitement, and the vast quantities of the region's red, white, and rosé wines that flow from cask and carafe at every corner.

RIGHT *The lithe, white-garbed* raseteurs *(bull-chasers) who try to pluck the valuable* cocardes *(pom-poms), from between the bulls' horns at a bullfight in Mouriès have to be quick on—and off—their feet.* OPPOSITE TOP *The traditional Farandole dance, performed by dancers in regional costumes, is one of the highlights of Mouriès's Fête aux Olives Vertes.* BELOW LEFT *A small museum at the Marius Fabre factory traces the art and craft of Provençal soap-making.* BELOW RIGHT *Chunky blocks of olive oil–based soap, a fixture at every Provençal kitchen sink, emerge daily from the traditional molds of the Fabre factory, in business for more than a hundred years.*

ARMA

PHARMACIE

FONDÉE EN 1775

LES VERTS

LEFT *Complementing an early-20th-century portrait, which was discovered in a local flea market, are very subtle green-hued taupe walls of La Grenache, a guest house on the grounds of the Bastide de Marie in Ménèrbes.* RIGHT *A pea-green door at an antique home in the Vaucluse harmonizes with the old stonework of the facade.* OPPOSITE, CLOCKWISE FROM TOP LEFT *In a small salon of painter Hervé Thibault's home in the Luberon, a panoply of greens embellishes not only the rare 18th-century commode from Aix-en-Provence, but the walls, a night table, and the sconces as well; green-on-green is the color choice of an old pharmacy in Barjols, in the Haut Var; a bedroom of La Grenache glows with luminous pale green walls; an emerald-green art deco plate from the Pichon atelier in Uzès commemorates the region's famous Roman bridge, the Pont du Gard.*

olives themselves, like the luscious hue of little, brine-cured picholines. Many other greens also enhance both the landscape and regional decorative style, among them the deep green of soaring cypresses, planted in close formation as windbreaks; the grayed green of wild thyme; the soft, dusty green of almond trees in Lower Provence; and the vivid green of garden-fresh basil. Greens appear as often as blues in cheerful window and door trims on colorful facades, creating a harmonious link between house and garden.

Finally, there is **white.** An achromatic color, but a color nonetheless, white is as intrinsic to the style of Provence as the vivid ochers, pinks, blues, yellows, and greens. White is the color of the pristine bridal *boutis* (quilts) stitched to cover the nuptial bed; it is the color of beautiful and rare Moustiers faience; and it is a color that especially marks the Camargue: the muscular white Camarguais horses; the tall white mountains of salt processed and stored at waterside saltworks in Salin-

🌊 LES BLANCS

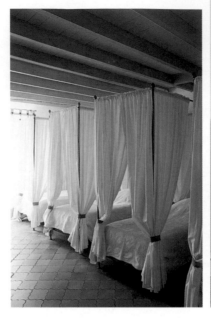

🐚 LEFT *A demure lineup of four single canopy beds fills La Chambre des Nonnes (the "Nun's Room") at the Maison de la Source in Lauris.* RIGHT *A well-used hat rack is a magnet for family chapeaux in the white-washed entrance hall of an artist's home near Bonnieux.* OPPOSITE, CLOCKWISE FROM TOP LEFT *The dazzling white horses of the Camargue, a breed unto themselves, graze placidly in the fields near Le Sambuc; salvaged moldings frame the curtained bathtub of an airy tiled bathroom at the Bastide de Moustiers; for the living room of an elegant bastide in the Luberon, decorator Bruno Lafourcade chose a serene palette of cream and gray; in April, an orchard of cherry trees near Roussillon burst into snowy bloom; a sign on the door to the sought-after White Bedroom—"La Blanche"—at Alain Ducasse's Bastide de Moustiers, bids guests to pause and listen to the song of the cicadas.* 🐚

de-Giraud; and, most dramatically, the dazzling whitewashed ranches and thatch-roofed *cabanons* (waterside cottages). White, in fact, was also the interior wall color of most Provençal homes until the mid-20th century, before the yellows, pinks, greens, and blues came indoors. In the old days, interior walls were white-washed and touches of color came mainly from brightly printed fabric on cushions and curtains, or perhaps a piece or two of painted furniture. Some traditional homes have never given up their matte white interiors, while among trend-setters, white is making a stylish return in walls—tiled or painted—and sheer white curtains that softly filter the bright sunlight. Bright touches of true color are bestowed once again by accents such as pillows, cushions, furniture, and paintings. In some homes, however, even the wood trim and accents are painted in neutrals, in beige or taupe, or even more fashionably in shades of soft gray—popular in 18th-century provincial style—creating an interior that is cool, luminescent, and serene.

La Blanche

Laissez-nous écouter les cigales

LA BASTIDE DE MOUSTIERS
04360 Moustiers-Sainte-Marie
Tel : 04 92 70 47 47 - Fax : 04 92 70 47 48
http://www.bastide-moustiers.i2m.fr
e-mail : bastide@i2m.fr

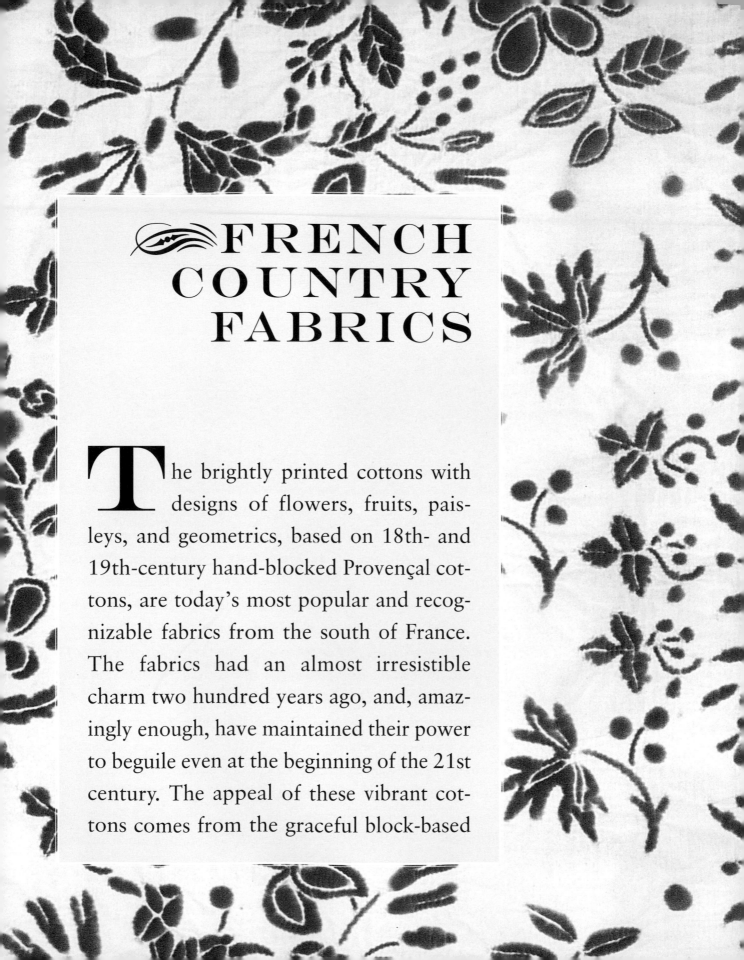

FRENCH COUNTRY FABRICS

The brightly printed cottons with designs of flowers, fruits, paisleys, and geometrics, based on 18th- and 19th-century hand-blocked Provençal cottons, are today's most popular and recognizable fabrics from the south of France. The fabrics had an almost irresistible charm two hundred years ago, and, amazingly enough, have maintained their power to beguile even at the beginning of the 21st century. The appeal of these vibrant cottons comes from the graceful block-based

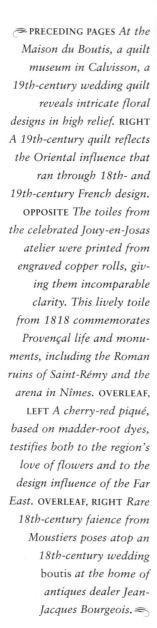
prints, a curious mélange of naïveté and sophistication, and from the warm and varied colorations, which range from subdued to vivid. The high-grade cotton fabrics were printed with vegetable dyes, which gave great character and a spectrum of subtle hues to the prints. In the old days, through the early 1900s, fabrics were produced primarily in three varieties: the *enluminés,* brightly colored for girls and young women; the *grisailles,* in muted, grayed colorations for women "of a certain age"; and the *deuils,* somber-toned patterns for elderly women and widows.

These seminal fabrics did not spring full-blown from the imaginations of Provençal artisans. Rather, these artisans were themselves inspired by the stunningly printed cottons brought into the port of Marseille in the mid-17th century aboard the great ships of the Compagnie des Indes Orientales. The arrival of these vivid fabrics dazzled the French with their intricate patterns and striking tones, and they became a *succès fou* in Paris and at the court of Versailles. The event

marked not only the beginning of Western fascination with brightly printed cottons, but indeed the birth of the modern cotton industry in France. The French called the fabrics *calicots* (for Calcutta), *chints* (from the Hindu word for the cotton fabrics), or simply *indiennes*.

In the late 17th century, French textile producers set up ateliers to produce their own *indiennes*, a new industry that drew artisans and other textile workers away from the silk and wool factories of Lyon. It took many decades for the French to develop the expertise and technical know-how to create high-quality printed cottons. Particularly challenging was developing the technique for making the fabrics colorfast; the secret, the French ultimately learned, was in the mordants—metallic salts that combined with dyes to form an insoluble compound on natural fibers. It wasn't until the second half of the 18th century that the French were capable of producing superbly printed cottons, which were Indian-inspired but reflected the colors and flora of the regions in which they were manufactured. For the next one hundred years the *indiennes* remained secure in their popularity, although styles and tastes changed. Under Louis XV, who reigned from 1774 to 1791, flower, vine, and herb prints on a bronze-hued background, dubbed *"les bonnes herbes,"* were in vogue. This was followed by a passion for geometrics—squares, stripes, and ovals—during the short Directoire period, which lasted from 1795 to 1799. Later, during the reign of Napoléon in the early 1800s, the fashion crowd had a penchant for tiny intricate patterns called *milles raies, pois,* and *petits cercles.*

During the heyday of these dainty prints, another genre of printed cotton was coming to the fore. These were the toiles, on heavier, linen-textured cottons, with elaborate, more graphic, monochromatic prints in red, blue, gold, brown, or black on an off-white background. Toiles had elegant patterns that often celebrated pastoral landscapes or allegorical scenes, or paid homage to historical events or local monuments. In the north, outside of Paris in the town of Jouy-en-Josas, the company of Christophe-Philippe Oberkampf was creating lavishly patterned toiles de Jouy. Lesser known, but equally handsome, were the toiles d'Aix, which were being produced in superb colorations, such as mauve

OPPOSITE, CLOCKWISE FROM TOP LEFT *Two graceful 18th-century toiles d'Aix (toile fabrics created in Aix-en-Provence), live again in these stylish reproductions from Les Olivades; Florence Maeght has long loved and collected 18th- and 19th-century Provençal quilts, a passion that eventually grew into her business, Le Rideau de Paris, which offers high-quality reproductions, among them this floral beauty on a Turkish-red background; extraordinary quilting work went into the creation of* boutis, *such as these romantic 18th-century specimens, in which the white ground clearly shows the neat, sensuously curved and gently raised pattern—each row filled with cotton; in this collection of 18th- and 19th-century Provençal petticoats, the embroidery work combines techniques of traditional quilting in the body, with finely worked,* boutis-*style hems.*

or rose, by several ateliers in Aix-en-Provence. The toiles d'Aix were snapped up by the local nobles and bourgeoisie to decorate the grand *bastides* (country estates) in and around Aix.

One of the most popular ways to make beautiful use of the captivating Provençal cottons—both the block-printed florals and paisleys and, to a lesser degree, the elegant toiles d'Aix—was to stitch them up into eye-catching quilts. These treasured creations were often the centerpiece of the country bedroom. Provençal quilts divide into two very distinct categories: the *piqués* and the *boutis*. The *piqués* are what we usually think of as quilts, in which two pieces of cotton sandwich a soft, fibrous filling and are then stitched together in an intricate design. The *boutis* are elaborate, all-white marriage quilts, created as part of a

OPPOSITE An imposing early-19th-century armoire holds a fraction of André Cabanel's enviable quilt collection. OVERLEAF In what once served as his living room, Cabanel's ever-growing horde of antique quilts covers every available surface.

ANDRÉ CABANEL'S QUILT COLLECTION

One of the world's best collections of antique *piqué* quilts resides with a man named André Cabanel in a small village west of Nîmes. Mr. Cabanel became enamored of these quilts—their colors, their patterns, their history—in the early 1960s, after he returned home from his military service. "We had a few in our family," he remembers, "and, you know, when you have a few examples of something wonderful, you tend to start to want a few more." He began haunting the local flea markets and found superb quilts for a pittance. He even found them for nothing at local dumps. "People sometimes thought of these old quilts as rags, old junk. They wanted new, modern things, not these frumpy old cloths." Over the next several decades Mr. Cabanel, a farmer by vocation, made hay while the sun shone, so to speak. His collection of quilts—both *piqués* and *boutis*—from the 18th and 19th centuries numbers in the hundreds and fills almost every room in his house from floor to ceiling. His quilts have been featured in museum shows, and recently a selection of his prized *piqués* was chosen by the fabric company Brunswig & Fils to be reproduced as the André Cabanel collection.

ABOVE André Cabanel inspects one of his lovely prize quilts, this one from the 19th century.

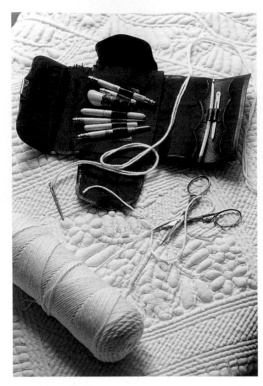

bride's trousseau. The *boutis* were much more labor-intensive than the *piqués*. To create a *boutis,* designs—perhaps a rose, a heart, or a ribbed border—were stitched into a double layer of fine white cotton, and then each little bit of the design was individually stuffed with cotton wool or batting through a tiny hole left in the design. After each motif was stuffed and then stitched closed, the creator would go on to the next little motif. A small *boutis* would take at least two thousand hours to create. For this reason, *boutis* are today quite rare on the market, and extremely expensive. The *piqués,* while less demanding to make, are also very beautiful, and fine antique specimens, quite recherché, are expensive when you find them in good antiques markets or from top dealers such as Bruno Carles in Lunel and Michel Biehn in L'Isle-sur-la-Sorgue.

By the middle of the 19th century, with the burgeoning of the Industrial Revolution, the hand-printed cotton industry in Provence and elsewhere went into decline. Many small producers who had worked *à la planche*—block by block—sold out to or joined the great industrial fabric producers who printed by machine. Great collections of carved blocks were burned as detritus of another age. Only in areas removed from the industrial mainstream—notably Lower Provence and Alsace—did a few companies continue to hand-print cottons for regional costumes.

The renaissance of the Provençal cotton industry in the 20th century was due mainly to Charles Deméry, a visionary who in 1938 took over the creaky old fabric company of an uncle, also called Charles Deméry, which had roots back to the late 1700s. The company headquarters in

ABOVE A 19th-century quilter's kit for creating the white boutis de mariage *(bridal quilt) rests on a* boutis *of the same era at the Maison du Boutis in Calvisson.* OPPOSITE *A 19th-century marriage* boutis *displays the intricate, romantic embroidered relief patterns characteristic of the genre, including a neoclassic vase full of flowers, symbolizing abundance.*

Tarascon, a small city on the Rhône south of Avignon, had in its dusty attics a phenomenal collection of more than forty thousand carved and laminated fruitwood blocks, carefully stacked and documented. Out of this collection came a rare working library of prints for the company that Mr. Deméry renamed Souleiado, a Provençal word meaning sunshine streaming through the clouds. Souleiado, in the years after World War II, went on to introduce these beautiful fabrics around the world. In the early years, Souleiado continued to print fabric the old-fashioned way, by hand, meter by meter. But by the late 1940s, as demand for their fabrics increased, the company could no longer continue to print fabrics by hand. It was also at this time that vegetable dyes had given way to high-quality synthetic dyes. From the 1950s on, Souleiado began the slow transition to printing fabrics industrially, on engraved copper rolls. For the highest degree of authenticity possible, designs were transferred onto copper plates complete with some imperfections—cracks or scrapes—from the original wood blocks.

Today, several companies, which either followed in the footsteps of Charles Deméry or were quietly producing cottons all along in regional

LEFT A large, intricately worked fruitwood planche (printing block) is part of the massive collection of 18th- and 19th-century hand-carved blocks in the archives of the Souleiado Museum in Tarascon. Almost all of today's Provençal fabrics are based, at least in part, on elements from 17th-, 18th-, and 19th-century fabric design. RIGHT An atmospheric old workroom at the Souleiado headquarter is now part of the company's intriguing museum. OPPOSITE A 20th-century fabric at the Souleiado Museum, hand-printed from antique blocks, uses old design elements to contemporary effect.

ateliers, continue the tradition of the great Provençal *cotonniers*. One of the best these days is Les Olivades, a company in Saint-Etienne-du-Grès that was founded in 1818 and has been owned by the same family, the Boudins, since 1948. Les Olivades, which presents new collections every season while maintaining its popular classics, grows increasingly strong in terms of quality, design, and scope of production. Other fine companies include Valdrôme, in the Drôme, and Le Mistral, based in Nîmes. Together the companies offer hundreds of different design and color combinations, many in the vivid, traditional colors of Provence, others in newer, more sophisticated shades of moss, grège, grape, amber, pale wheat, smoky gray, and dusty rose. There are always new fabrications coming out of these companies, particularly Les Olivades and Souleiado, but most, although contemporary in spirit, are still based on patterns from antique blocks. The designs are usually compositions, taking, for example, the pinpoint background from one block, a floral accent strip from another block, a paisley center from a third, and perhaps a scalloped garland from a fourth.

Among the most recent fabric innovations from today's Provençal *cotonniers* are the beautiful reproductions of the classic toiles d'Aix from Les Olivades. Produced in contemporary hues of mauve, ripe wheat, antique gray, cinnabar red, and cerulean blue, the elegant and sophisticated fabrics give a new perspective to historic Provençal cottons, normally perceived simply as winsome and merry. Among the patterns are scenes of goddesses with naughty cupids, and striking 18th-century floral still lifes.

Provençal cottons have enjoyed a remarkable success over the past fifty years, especially so in the past two decades. Perhaps the most compelling reason is that the patterns and colors are so compatible, whether they are combined among themselves, say a Provençal pastiche of two or three small prints plus a wider border print, or used in other, oftentimes quite diverse décors, from contemporary designs in neutral hues to lavish Oriental environments. Whether the setting is purely Provençal, Malibu Moderne, or Park Avenue penthouse, Provençal cottons endow the décor with a warmth and charm unique to the Midi.

OPPOSITE Florence Maeght uses her vast collection of antique Provençal quilts to create stunning reproductions, such as this beautiful, two-patterned 19th-century-style quilt, for her Paris shop, Le Rideau de Paris.

FURNITURE OF PROVENCE

From voluminous armoires to tiny étagères, the Provençal cabinet-maker's exuberance, love of movement, and passion for detail shine through in every undulating line, every sinuous curve, every little carved fish and flower. The artisans of Provence—a diverse group ranging from simple carpenters and former ship chandlers to highly trained cabinetmakers—used every opportunity to express themselves and display their skill. And yet, they never lost sight of

PRECEDING PAGES *A rare 18th-century Louis XVI radassier (rush-seated Provençal banquette), with its original paint, was discovered by antiques dealer Jean-Jacques Bourgeois at a bastide near Saint-Raphaël. The swags and acanthus leaf decoration are charming, rustic interpretations of Louis XVI style. An 18th-century quilt from Avignon forms the backdrop.* CLOCKWISE, FROM TOP LEFT *This 18th-century panetière (bread box), carved with a miller figure, presides over the dining room of Provençal poet Frédéric Mistral, whose home is now a museum in Maillane; a Louis XVI verrier (glass cabinet) adds charm to antiques dealer Bruno Carles's kitchen; adorning the kitchen of the Mas de Peint are a quaint* farinière *and* salière *(flour box and salt box); in the workroom of antiques dealer Frédéric Dervieux, a* farinière *and* salière *await restoration.* OPPOSITE *A rustic 19th-century armoire from the Camargue, endearing with its humble renderings of swags and flowers, awaits a buyer at the Mas de Curebourg, in Isle-sur-la-Sorgue.*

practicality and comfort as their priorities. As a result, no furniture combines form and function more gracefully than those pieces that are designed in *le style provençal.*

The origins of some traditional Provençal furniture were very humble, most first created in rural farming areas by carpenters to fill a specific need: armoires and buffets to store linens and dishes away from the harvest dust; *garde-mangers* and *panetières* for storing food out of reach of rodents and other animals; the *pétrin* for kneading dough and storing it while it rose; and flour boxes, salt boxes, and a variety of little étagères for storing ingredients and tableware. Eventually each of

these rustic pieces evolved into expensively commissioned pieces by master cabinetmakers that would grace town houses, mansions, aristocratic and bourgeois country estates, and even châteaux.

The best Provençal furniture married the practical needs of the countryside with the imagination and expertise of the finest craftsmen, and the results were works of art. The utilitarian, which had its own unique, simple beauty, became elegant, even at times lavish, rendered in beautiful woods and often highly ornamented. Gentle, artfully curved lines, exquisitely carved floral detail, lacy ironwork, and deeply patinated woods define the finest Provençal armoires, buffets, credenzas, and *panetières*. In a land of brilliant sun, where light and shadow are sharply defined, artisans also adapted the natural chiaroscuro to their furniture, juxtaposing straight lines with curved, and deeply carved surfaces with mirror-smooth ones to catch and move the light.

The 17th and 18th centuries are the *grands siècles*—literally the "great centuries"—of French furniture design, in Provence particularly so. By the 17th century, regional schools of style developed, particularly in Avignon and to the southeast in Toulon and Marseille, where French naval officers and wealthy shipowners supported ateliers of furniture craftsmen. During the 18th century, an economically rich period for France, provincial design flourished throughout the country, and in Provence a trend toward opulent ornamentation bloomed. Provençal furniture makers responded immediately to the sensuous, lyrical elegance of Louis XV style, *Louis Quinze,* identifying with its expressive, generous lines and unrestrained romanticism. It was then, during the reign of Louis XV (1715–1774), that Provençal furniture took on the lines and forms that today most characterize the style.

Much of the best Provençal furniture from that time came from the Bouches-du-Rhône, a department in Lower Provence that hugs the eastern banks of the Rhône river. The land was fertile and profitable, and the locals prospered not only from this and the active river trade but also from an enormous international trade fair in Beaucaire—with buyers and sellers arriving by land, river, and sea—that thrived for seven hundred years. Residents of Arles, Beaucaire, and Tarascon could afford

OPPOSITE An imposing 18th-century painted bureau Avignonnais (desk from Avignon) commands a corner of a long, luminous gallery at the Abbaye Saint-André in Villeneuve-lès-Avignon. The elegant caned Louis XVI chairs with grid-patterned seats represent a style of chair crafted for aristocratic and wealthy bourgeois families of the period. Panels with bucolic country scenes embellish the 18th-century painted canvas Provençal screen to the left of the desk.

to pay more for fine furniture. And since the Bouches-du-Rhône was where the money was, that was also where the craftsmen gathered, not exclusively those from Provence, but those from Italy and Spain as well. Two major styles originating in this area were a powerful influence in Provençal furniture: the style of Arles and the style of Fourques.

While the forms or silhouettes of both styles are basically the same, the ornamentation is different. The furniture of Arles is the more elaborate, more highly worked, with ornately carved and curved lines and lavish floral detail. This style is sometimes called *fleuri* (flowered). Sinuous carved moldings characterize both styles, but in the Arlesian pieces, the emphasis is rather on the delicate, low-relief detail, such as garlands of roses, flower buds, and olive branches. Many experts credit the development of the Arlesian style to an 18th-century sculptor name Bernard Turau, who had embellished many of the finest homes in the region with swags, garlands, flowers, and shells, and who left behind him, as a legacy to all the local craftsmen, a rich archive of design notebooks. Furniture from nearby Fourques, a smaller, simpler town at the tip of the Camargue, has less carved detail and ornamentation; craftsmen there, influenced by the lines and movement of Louis XV style, specialized in deeply sculpted curves, volutes, and undulating moldings with little or no figurative detail. The effect is more vigorous, more architectural, and slightly more rustic that the Arlesian look.

Other important design centers were Uzès, which developed a distinctive style of elaborate, highly detailed painted furniture, or furniture decorated with découpage; Marseille, where wealthy and sophisticated shipowners with access to goods from all over the world commissioned Provençal-style furniture but had it crafted in exotic woods, such as rosewood, mahogany, and ebony; and Aix-en-Provence, where a moneyed and somewhat ostentatious bourgeoisie favored ornate furniture with a high degree of delicate detailing and refinement. Furniture design was of a dramatically different character in the northern reaches of Provence, in the austere, mountainous Comtat-Venaissin region. A stronghold of Protestants seeking refuge from the persecutions of the south, Haute

Provence (Upper Provence) was a rocky, bare-bones kind of place, and the rustic furniture created there reflects the restraint and practicality of the lifestyle. A minimum of decoration and squared silhouettes rather than sensuous Louis XV–style curves characterize the genre. What embellishments there were—large *points de diamants* (diamond patterns), for example—reflect the contained geometric influence of Louis XV's great-great-grandfather, Louis XIII, who reigned from 1610 to 1643.

Traditional Provençal furniture was crafted from a variety of woods, but by far the most characteristic is honey-toned golden walnut, a variety with a faint reddish hue that was once abundant in northern Provence but grew scarce years ago. The wood was cut in the forests of Haute Provence and the Dauphiné and then floated down the Rhône to the design centers of Lower Provence, such as Arles or Avignon. Walnut trees were always prized, and the wood—essential for creating the finest armoires—was often bought and set aside to age, in anticipation of crafting an armoire to be part of a bride's dowry years ahead of a potential wedding. Cabinetmakers loved working with walnut, a wood with a texture, density, and tone that responded eloquently to the craftsman's chisel and awl. To a lesser extent, furniture makers employed other woods: soft lime wood for mirrors (a specialty of Beaucaire); pear wood, tinted black to resemble ebony; olive wood; willow for chairs; chestnut, mulberry, and cherry, sometimes combined on a single piece of furniture; and occasionally pine, a humble wood that was often painted.

ABOVE *A rare and beautiful 18th-century folding table from Avignon sumptuously adorned with flowers was created more for decorative effect than practicality, perhaps adding color and romance to a countess's boudoir.*

Classic Furniture of Provence

The cabinetmakers of Provence crafted furniture for each room of the house, even though the kitchen and the living room claimed the most important pieces. The kitchen, the heart of the Provençal home, inspired a good half-dozen, most of them unique to the region. The most distinctive, perhaps, is the *panetière*, an elaborately sculpted cage designed to store fresh bread. An elegant grillwork frame composed of *chandelles* (candlestick-like spindles symmetrically spaced all around) allowed the free flow of air. Bread was inserted and removed through a decoratively carved door—sometimes adorned with diminutive *ferrures* in the center of the grillwork. Elegantly carved *bobèches* crowned the top while tiny curved feet graced the bottom. The feet were initially intended to support the *panetière* on the top of a buffet or another piece of storage furniture, but it quickly became the custom, certainly by the early 19th century, to suspend the *panetière* from the kitchen wall, keeping the bread out of the reach of rodents and opening up more surface area on the buffet or credenza below. Displayed with pride as the centerpiece in many a Provençal kitchen, the *panetière* is a remarkable regional masterwork.

Traditionally, the *panetière* was placed above the **pétrin**, a sturdy, trough-like piece of furniture designed for the preparation of bread (*pétrir* means "to knead"). Often part of a bride's dowry, the *pétrin*, a trapezoidal chest with a hinged top, was used to knead dough and store it while it rose. A variety of bases were created to support the *pétrin*, the most characteristic being four sculpted legs joined by an ornately carved traverse. Simpler versions placed the *pétrin* atop a modest, two-drawered table. Images of flowers, olive branches, wheat sheaves, and miller's tools decorate the more elaborately worked *pétrins,* while others are adorned only with molding.

Also among the functional furnishings of a Provençal kitchen was the unusual **tamisadou**. Created to refine and sift flour, it was a two-door cabinet containing a *moulin à bluter* (bolting mill), which was used to separate out the bran, leaving the coarsely ground flour for cooking. There was originally an exterior handle on the right side, but it is very

OPPOSITE, CLOCKWISE FROM TOP LEFT *Crossed arrows and diamond motifs adorn the door of this unusual Directoire-style* panetière *from Jean-Jacques Bourgeois; Arles antiques dealer Frédéric Dervieux displays this distinctive, early-19th-century armoire from Fourques, with its deeply sculpted curved moldings and almost no figurative detail; from* antiquaire *Robert Reyre in Aix-en-Provence, this commode Arlésienne, crafted about 1859, is an elaborate 19th-century reproduction of an 18th-century piece; at the Frédéric Mistral Museum in Maillane, a late-18th-century* armoire de mariage, *graced with a carved pair of cooing doves, dominates the small bedroom of Madame Mistral.*

rare today to find one with its handle and mill intact. Most, having lost their inner workings long ago, serve today as buffets.

Another traditional piece crafted for the kitchen is the **garde-manger,** a food storage cabinet, usually tall and narrow in silhouette with an openwork facade covered with partial wooden grillwork resembling a *panetière*. Occasionally, the open area would be covered instead by fine-mesh screen. *Garde-mangers* typically have a single door and a small drawer on the bottom. Some rustic *garde-mangers* are bereft of decoration, while others are adorned with beautifully wrought hinges, *ferrures,* and elegant floral carving. Two of the smallest kitchen pieces are the *farinière* and the *salière,* or *boîte à sel,* decoratively carved boxes that usually hung from hooks on either side of the hearth. The *salière,* with a slanted, hinged top, was used for storing salt, while the *farinière,* with a sliding front panel, was used for storing flour, as well as for flouring fish.

The wall in the kitchen or dining area was also the repository for various types of small étagères, designed for very specific functions. The **vaisselier** held dishes, the **verrier** glassware, the **estagnié** pewter, and the **coutelière** knives. The étagères had in common carved shelf fronts that retain the displayed objects, but other characteristics vary. Some pieces have fabric-covered backs to enhance the display, while others are backless, creating an airier, more delicate piece especially suitable for displaying glasses. Similar to the *panetière,* many were created with tiny feet that were virtually never used, since the étagères were attached to a wall. Some étagères, rare and beautiful, mimic the lines and decoration of an armoire, with undulating cornices, extravagantly carved motifs, tiny doors, and equally tiny *ferrures.*

The Provençal piece of furniture that claims pride of place in any traditional home is the imposing and often elaborately carved **armoire.** A substantial storage cabinet that can soar to as high as 10 feet tall, the armoire, usually fashioned out of walnut, was traditionally crafted with two doors, two to three carved panels per door, and ornate *ferrures* trimming the edges of each door. The most characteristic cornice, particularly on armoires whose provenance is Lower Provence, is the

OPPOSITE Set in the corner of a farmer's kitchen, this elegant Provençal garde-manger (food storage cabinet) from Nîmes was created and signed in 1789, a momentous year for France. It has lavish, lacy ferrures (ironwork), grillwork of superbly carved spindles, and intricately carved motifs that were popular during the reign of Louis XVI, such as the exquisite open-work soupière (tureen) below the doors.

MOTIFS AND METALLIC DETAILING

A wide range of romantic and symbolic motifs adorn Provençal furniture, expressing both the region's and the particular craftsman's joie de vivre. Motifs reflecting conjugal love embellish armoires and other furniture that comprised a bride's dowry, or that were offered as wedding gifts. Predominant, of course, are hearts, sometimes touching or interlocked, as well as eglantine flowers and myrtle leaves. Prosperity and abundance were represented by sheaves of wheat and bunches of grapes, while vines conveyed the wish and hope for longevity. Floral designs were often carved into glowing walnut or fruitwood, including bouquets of Provençal flowers, acanthus leaves, almond branches, pinecones, ears of corns, and marguerites. Nonbotanical motifs include harvest tools, carafes, fish (often gracing small flour boxes used to coat fish fillets), and soup tureens, a symbol of the family dinner. More sophisticated, court-influenced motifs became fashionable during the reign of Louis XVI and Marie Antoinette, monarchs who favored furniture adorned with ribbons, garlands of pearls, cockle shells, and musical instruments.

Another characteristic decorative element on some of the finest Provençal furniture—particularly on pieces created in the Bouches-du-Rhône region—are the lacy, symmetrical *ferrures,* handsomely wrought and polished iron- or steelwork. The thin, delicately wrought, shining *ferrures* are another element that—like the chiaroscuro carving on armoires and cabinets that play with light and shadow—used light, in this case reflected, to decorative advantage. Typically, this elegant metalwork, a legacy of the expert blacksmiths from Spain who made their way into Provence looking for work in the late 17th and early 18th centuries, adorned the doors of armoires and buffets. The *ferrures,* used in pairs or even trios, were set along the entire length of a door's inside edge.

ABOVE *Sumptuously carved flowers, quivers, and arrows embellish a rare 18th-century* litoche *(Provençal bed) at the Vincent Mît L'Ane shop.* LEFT *Decorative metal* ferrures *take advantage of the play of light and shadow.* OPPOSITE *Some elegant* armoires de mariage *were adorned with the carved monogram of the bride. The handsomely wrought monogram on this 18th-century armoire is draped with ribbons and acanthus leaves, popular motifs during the reign of Louis XVI.*

distinctive *chapeau de gendarme* ("policeman's hat" style), which is flat on either end and arched in the center. Supporting the armoire are feet in one of three forms: *escargot* (snail), *corne de bélier* (ram's horn), or *pied de biche* (doe's hoof). The finest armoires are richly carved in high relief, or even open-work detailing, featuring romantically symbolic motifs of doves, hearts, torches, or flowers.

As grandiose and opulent as some armoires can be, certainly not all fall into this category. Many armoires were quite humble, crafted for families of very modest means who saved their sous for many years to be able to commission the piece and present it to a daughter on the occasion of her marriage. The armoire often became a family's most valuable possession, passed down from one generation to the next as a treasured heirloom. All authentic Provençal armoires these days are rare and costly, with those from Arles, Saint Rémy, Avignon, Aix-en-Provence, Fourques, or Beaucaire among the most recherché. If you are lucky enough to discover a fine specimen in the antiques markets of Provence, it may well still be lined inside with antique *indienne* cottons, a practical touch that brightened the armoire's somber interior.

A unique two-tiered cabinet, the **buffet-à-glissants** is another striking example of the Provençal cabinetmaker's artistry. In this piece, often commissioned by aristocratic or *hautes bourgeoises* families, a buffet bottom with two sculpted doors topped by a long drawer is crowned by a smaller, separate recessed tier. This upper tier was crafted with two sliding panels (*glissants*), often ornately carved and equipped with wrought-iron pulls. The sliding panels flanked a small central storage compartment called a *tabernacle*—where small statues of saints, rosaries, and other religious items were often stored—accessed by a small carved door. With the well-conceived design of the *buffet-à-glissants,* you could store and retrieve glassware or dishes while leaving large tureens and vases placed on the buffet top undisturbed.

A variation of the two-tiered buffet theme is the large and often majestically proportioned **buffet-à-deux-corps** (chest-on-chest). In this distinctive, and perhaps counterintuitive piece, the slightly recessed top portion, with two tall cabinet doors, is often twice as high as the lower

OPPOSITE, CLOCKWISE FROM TOP LEFT *A graceful 18th-century commode from Nîmes is crowned by an ornate 18th-century mirror from Beaucaire, a town once famed for its elegantly carved and gilded mirrors, and an armillary-style contemporary lamp by Paris designer Jean Reverdy; a late-18th-century* pétrin *from Arles, in the shop of Nathalie Légier in L'Isle-sur-la-Sorgue, displays small period collectibles, among them a dainty* sal-ière *(salt box), a* coutelière *(knife holder), and a tall glazed pitcher called a* Démoiselle d'Avignon; *elegant asymmetrical doors, lavish* ferrures, *intricate carving on every possible surface, and classic feet à l'escargot* distinguish this *early 19th-century* buffet-à-glissants *in the collection of antique dealer Frédéric Dervieux; two armoire doors discovered at an architectural salvage company get a new lease on life as a* buffet-mural, *fronting a closet in a small bedroom near Grasse.*

supporting portion, which usually has two cabinet doors topped with two small drawers. Imposing in its dimensions, the *buffet-à–deux-corps* was often very restrained in décor, adorned perhaps simply with a *chapeau de gendarme* cornice. The **buffet-crédence** (credenza) is a low traditional buffet, more ornate than the *buffet-à-deux-corps,* with cabinet doors often decorated with arches, small *ferrures,* and doors with recessed framed panels surrounded by molding. Some *buffet-crédences* are topped with beautiful pink or gray marble from the region. An early example of built-ins with a buffet theme is the **buffet-mural** (wall buffet), a wall-storage unit set into the wall with a buffet or armoire fade. The *buffet-mural* can vary dramatically in size, some small versions tuck into a corner of a room, while large versions can dominate an entire wall. In many fine home restorations these days, homeowners in Provence are creating updated versions of *buffet-murals* on living room or bedroom walls out of armoire doors they find at regional flea markets. The additions showcase an attractive and practical way to use the antique "leftovers," often attractively priced, that abound in flea markets and architectural salvage firms throughout France.

Every room has corners, and often corners are simply lost space, not suited for furniture. But canny Provençal craftsmen conceived a solution for the lost corner, and called it an **encoignure.** This practical and distinctly regional piece was a long, narrow, three-sided cabinet designed to fit precisely in a corner, with sides that taper to a point in the back. Some *encoignures* have straight fronts, others are bowed, ornamented sparingly with deeply carved molding or scrollwork and small *ferrures.*

As inspired as Provençal furniture makers were in creating armoires, buffets, and étagères, they were surprisingly uninspired in designing and building **dining tables.** Functional and utilitarian, the dining table apparently did not capture the fancy of the Provençal craftsman, or, perhaps more to the point, the fancy of the craftsmen's clientele. Antique Provençal tables are generally long and rectangular—some could seat up to twelve diners—simple and solid but not particularly interesting. Some tables had drawers on either end for holding flatware and napkins. If an original, unrestored 17th- or 18th-century table

should appear on the market now—a rare event—the table would most likely be too low for today's diners, crafted as it was in an age when people were generally shorter. Although dining tables were constructed plainly, Provençal carpenters concentrated their artistic efforts in crafting smaller tables—game tables, writing tables, dressing tables, hall tables—for more affluent abodes. Sleek and elegant, these pieces are marked not by carved detail but by the striking curves of their legs.

Chairs and banquettes, on the other hand, reflect a great deal of regional style, although most are primarily rustic, with an emphasis on comfort and practicality rather than adornment. The rush-seated banquette (*radassier*) is the most characteristic seat in the house. Designed to accommodate three or occasionally four people, the *radassier* was traditionally placed near the fireplace for chatting, knitting, or quilting before or after dinner. For the *radassier,* as well as in the regional chairs and fauteuils, seat bottoms were woven of natural rush, or of natural rush and tinted rush combined in a simple pattern. The fibers for the weaving came from the pale green reeds gathered in the marshes of the

LEFT *A small, charming* encoignure *(corner buffet cabinet) expertly repainted in a soft, mottled lime, fits neatly in the corner of a kitchen near Gordes.* RIGHT *A majestic, bow-fronted* encoignure *chest-on-chest was once part of a long enfilade of cabinets in a château, all painted in a golden walnut faux-bois.*

CLOCKWISE, FROM TOP LEFT *An unusual rush-woven shelf adds a touch of style to a humble 19th-century fruitwood side table; the allure of this graceful little Provençal desk lies in the sensuous Louis XV–style lines of its base; this elegant Louis XVI marble-topped demi-lune console table was designed in Aix-en-Provence for one of the city's grand bastides; a rare Louis XV table de curé was designed with a coin-slot in the center to make an offering after a visit to the village priest.* OPPOSITE *In the living room of the Frédéric Mistral house, an early-19th-century rolltop desk once belonging to the poet Lamartine sits beneath an imposing portrait of Mistral.*

Camargue, or from the strawlike grasses harvested from the banks of the Rhône. The frames were fashioned from traditional walnut, as well as from beech, linden, mulberry, or willow.

The banquette was simply designed, with three or four linked rush-seated chair bottoms, an arm on either end, and gently concave seat backs, sometimes adorned with carved flowers or olive branches. If crafted from walnut, the banquette would be left its natural color and polished with beeswax. But when constructed in other woods, the banquette would be among the few pieces of Provençal furniture that was routinely painted, usually in muted shades of gray, olive green, or gray-blue.

The design and construction of traditional chairs and armchairs was virtually identical to that of banquettes, although proportions and décor could vary substantially. There are well-proportioned armchairs called *fauteuils à la bonne femme,* designed—it is said—for grand-mothers who were left to tend the hearth. A very distinctive regional chair is called a *chaise de nourrice* (wet nurse's chair) with a very high back and a low seat, designed for a new mother or a wet nurse to suckle a baby. In general, seat backs on chairs were slatted and unadorned until the late 1770s, when, influenced by the style of Louis XVI, they became more stylized, with an upper and lower traverse bordering an elegant framed motif, such as a *montgolfier* (hot-air balloon), a sheaf of wheat (*à la gerbe*), or a gracefully carved lyre.

Several fine old firms today continue the tradition of crafting rush-bottomed chairs and banquettes, among them René Lacroix and the Monleau family, both located in the small town of Vallabrègues, near the banks of the Rhône south of Avignon.

Commodes, small, elegant walnut dressers in a variety of styles, were almost exclusively luxury items in the 18th and 19th centuries, commissioned by well-to-do families for the bedrooms or living rooms of their châteaux or *bastides.* They were produced primarily in three distinct styles: with three drawers, posed on short *escargot* or *pied de biche* feet; with two drawers set on long, gracefully curved legs, called *sauteuses* (literally "jumpers," since the legs look poised to spring into

OPPOSITE, CLOCKWISE FROM TOP LEFT *A modest sign points the way to the Monleau Company, a family of chair-makers in Vallabrègues that dates back to the late 19th century; a painted neoclassical panel adds personality to this Directoire chair from the late 1790s; delicately crafted sheaves of wheat—a popular Provençal motif—add a light and graceful touch to a pair of fruitwood side chairs from the 1830s; today off-limits to visitors, this lovely Louis XV banquette à trois places once welcomed guests in Frédéric Mistral's dining room in Maillane.*

the air); and, rarely, with a single drawer set on long, elegant legs, called a *perruquière* (wig-holder). The facades of commodes were often sensuously bowed, and were sometimes so ornately carved that they bordered on the baroque. The Provençal commode's elegant hardware usually has a golden hue, and was generally fashioned from copper or bronze.

Bedrooms, until just very recently, were never a focus of much design attention in Provence. Even today, bedrooms are often kept quite simple, in luxurious estate properties as well as in more modest farmhouses. Bedrooms might be equipped with no more than a small armoire, a chair, and a bed. The Provençal bed itself, called a **litoche,** is a modest creation with an arching, gently scalloped headboard and spare posts at the foot. If you should come across a more elaborately crafted antique *litoche* with a footboard higher than the headboard, most likely it would have been crafted in Arles. Toward the middle of the 19th century, during the reign of Napoléon III (1852–1870), a few very rich households, enchanted by the style dictates of the emperor and his fashionable wife, the Empress Eugénie, commissioned *lits à l'impériale* (canopy beds) with silk curtains suspended from a dome attached to the wall or ceiling. These days, an exception to the predominantly simple bed—and a recent innovation that could signal greater attention to bedroom décor—is the **ciel de lit.** This features a delicate wrought-iron "crown" installed on the wall or ceiling about six or seven feet above the head of the bed, something of a poor man's *lit*

ABOVE *Graceful sauteuse-style legs give a lift to this feminine 18th-century Arlesian commode displayed beneath a collection of vintage straw hats at the Fragonard Museum in Grasse.* OPPOSITE *A wrought-iron ciel-de-lit with sheer voile curtains adds a romantic touch to the bedroom of an elegant farmhouse in Eygalières.*

à l'impériale. Suspended from the *ciel de lit* are sheer voile curtains that fall around the bed like a veil. The look is romantic and feminine, and is appearing more and more often in some of the regions most charming inns and bed-and-breakfasts.

Traditions Continue

Provençal craftsmen and cabinetmakers continued creating furniture after the 18th century, certainly, but the furniture was never as beautiful and distinctive as it was in the glory years of the 17th and 18th century *grands siècles*. Nineteenth-century furniture makers in the region did produce some pieces in the styles of Charles X and Louis-Philippe, but by mid-century they focused increasingly on reproducing copies of 18th-century designs. This is why today, in many regional antique shops, you will find lovely Louis XV or Louis XVI–style armoires, buffets, or commodes that were crafted a century later than the originals, in the mid- to late 1800s. The turn of the 19th century, with the advent of mass-produced furniture from the north, marked the decline of Provençal regional style and, indeed, the demise of French provincial design in general.

Authentic, high-quality French antiques are becoming more and more difficult to find in France. The attics of everyone's dear old *tantes* and *grand-mères* are pretty much picked clean, and dealers bemoan the dearth of newly discovered antique items offered for sale. Most of what's out there recirculates in the market, at prices that spiral ever upward. To fill the void and respond to the ever-increasing demand for 18th- and 19th-century–style Provençal furniture, some of the region's most respected antiques dealers have developed their own handcrafted collections of line-for-line reproductions using old techniques and classic aged woods. Among the best of the classic copies are those offered by Bruno Carles in Lunel, Frédéric Dervieux in Arles, and Jean-Jacques Bourgeois—under the name Vincent Mit l'Âne—in L'Isle-sur-la-Sorgue. Today even the region's most glamorous houses proudly display handsomely crafted reproductions—often commissioned from photos in design books—among the antiques.

⌇ OPPOSITE A wonderful reproduction of a Louis XVI Provençal fauteuil by Vincent Mît L'Ane happily coexists with 18th-century originals at the home of Jean-Jacques Bourgeois. A Pierre Frey fabric called "Quai Voltaire," inspired by an 18th-century painted toile, covers the back and seat cushions. ⌇

PROVENÇAL POTTERY

The long, distinguished heritage of beautiful Provençal ceramics has its roots, appropriately enough, in the earth. The topography of Provence is richly larded with large deposits of high-quality clay, pink or red mostly, but occasionally white, a natural resource that from the time of the Roman Empire inspired a vast production of handmade earthenware and faience: pots, vases, pitchers, plates, cups, *santons* (the little Provençal crèche figures), and all kinds of

tiles. From the 17th century, ceramics ateliers flourished from the mountains of northern Provence south to the sea. They centered in towns that grew up near the clay deposits: Aubagne, Apt, Moustiers-Sainte-Marie, Dieulefit, Salernes, Varages, Biot, Vallauris, and west across the Rhône in Uzès and Anduze. There were also celebrated ateliers in Marseille, but most didn't survive beyond the end of the 18th century.

From the mundane pitcher and basin to decorative urns large enough to hold an orange tree, flowing graceful lines mark the traditional pottery of Provence. Depending upon the item's eventual shape, the clay is either molded or hand-thrown. For a characteristic octagonal or gently fluted plate or bowl, the clay is pressed into a classic mold fashioned from an 18th-century original. Hollowware—pitchers and vases, for example—are thrown and formed on a potter's wheel. Decorative detailing such as a bunch of grapes or a little serpent are always hand-sculpted and attached before firing.

The most traditional glazes you will see throughout Provence are a luminous mustard yellow that almost seems to glow from within; a deep, rich emerald green; and an opaque white used as the base for a variety of polychrome motifs. For the unusual marbled *terre-melée* (mixed-earth) faience of Apt and to a lesser degree Uzès, the glaze is

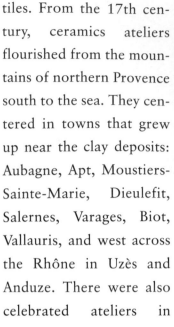

PRECEDING PAGES Soft, sensuous curves characterize both this 18th-century yellow platter from Apt and the dozen freshly gathered eggs it holds. ABOVE RIGHT *A 1950s Majolica-style cheese platter from Vallauris, mimicking a bamboo cheese mat, offers an assortment of ripe Provençal cheeses at a Sunday lunch.* BELOW RIGHT *The renowned turn-of-the-19th-century ceramist Louis Sicard was the first to make the cicada (shown here in glazed ceramics outside the Sicard atelier in Aubagne), a trendy Provençal design motif.* OPPOSITE *The Poterie Ravel in Aubagne, one of France's premier pottery towns, has been producing rosé-pink terra-cotta pots from custom-mixed local clays since 1837.*

clear, to better show off the beautiful swirling multicolored clays beneath. While each traditional pottery center creates its own distinct style of ceramics—Dieulefit specializes in rustic glazed earthenware and Anduze is famed for its giant glazed 18th-century-style garden pots, for example—two Provençal villages in particular have gained stellar international reputations that exceed the others, promulgated in part by regular editorial attention in travel and style publications: the villages of Moustiers and Apt.

Since the 16th century, Moustiers had been a village of potters with ample supplies of fine pink clay almost at their feet, but it took Pierre Clérissy, a man descended from a noted family of potters, to fire up the production of faience into an important local industry after he established his pottery atelier in 1679. By the late 18th century, faienceries developed a wide range of polychrome glazes. Moustiers's signature white glaze (with blue or green decorations) was originally developed to disguise the red clay underneath with an aim to making it look "finer" and more like porcelain. But the thick white glaze was never totally effective; somehow the pottery's vibrant pink heart managed to shine through, giving the faience of Moustiers its characteristic rosy glow.

Moustiers, one of the greatest centers historically, remains one of the most important faience centers in today's France. Pottery shops and ateliers line the steep little streets of this ancient village clinging to the cliffs in the Alpes-de-Haute-Provence region. The best producers of ceramics, such as the Atelier Soleil and the Atelier Bondil, follow ven-

ABOVE A 19th-century terre mélée (mixed-earth) vase from the Pichon atelier in Uzès and an early-20th-century Léo Lélée sketch of an Arlésienne keep company at the Souleiado Museum in Tarascon.
OPPOSITE Roseline Bacou's superb collection of 18th-century Marseille faience, adorned with characteristic florals, is displayed at the Abbaye de Saint-André in Villeneuve-lès-Avignon.

erable technical and artistic traditions, both in the way they work with the clay and in the motifs they use to adorn their faience. Signature motifs, many of which date from the 17th century, include *grotesques,* whimsical half-man, half-beast creatures that are distant cousins to the gargoyles of Nôtre Dame; scenes from mythology; *montgolfiers* (18th-century hot-air balloons); chinoiserie patterns; birds of paradise; and, after 1789, Revolutionary symbols and slogans. But Moustiers is not exclusivley lodged in the past. The best ateliers also feature contemporary designs, such as Atelier Soleil's vegetable, fruit, and fish designs by artist Florine Asch, and owner Franck Scherer's elegant contemporary plates with openwork pin-dots outlined in gold or platinum glaze circling the border. "We respect our ancestors and learn from them," says Scherer, the son of Tonya Peyrot, the former owner of Moustiers's renowned Atelier de Segriès, "but it is for us to mark the 20th and 21st centuries with our own designs, as our ancestors marked the 17th, 18th, and 19th centuries."

Another of France's most venerable and important faience centers, Apt, which thrived in the 18th and 19th centuries, now has only one major atelier to carry the standard and continue the tradition of its unique pottery: the proud, distinctive Atelier Bernard, now also called Faience d'Apt: Jean Faucon. In the late 1970s, the talented young *faiencier* Jean Faucon dedicated himself to continuing the work of his grandfather Joseph Bernard, who resurrected an all but lost 18th-century technique of creating faience from multicolored, marbleized clays. These pieces are not simply covered by a marbleized glaze; rather the intricately swirling patterns are in the clay itself—five different shades of clay, in fact—not just on the surface, but all the way through.

ABOVE A bull-themed art-deco plate from the Pichon atelier in Uzès embodies the atelier's distinctive design detailing: octagonal-sides, beaded borders, and jewel-toned glazes. OPPOSITE *The woven faience basket displays the Pichon atelier's characteristic little flowers ringing the basket's woven loops. The vintage faience is part of the Souleiado Museum collection in Tarascon.*

LEFT *At the Atelier Soleil in Moustiers, an artist uses a broad palette of colorful hues to decorate a group of traditional vases.* OPPOSITE, CLOCKWISE FROM TOP LEFT *A small "grotesque" figure plays the horn on a classic blue-and-white 18th-century Moustiers platter; a lively collection of little grotesques, revealing a Chinoiserie influence, romp across this 18th-century polychrome Moustier platter, while the two-tone plate above is a more subtle expression of the same genre and epoch; flowers adorn both a 19th-century Moustiers plate and a contemporary vintage-style fabric at the Souleidao headquaters in Tarascon; a trio of pitchers from different ateliers in Moustiers holds a home garden's harvest of fresh lavender in the Luberon.*

CLOCKWISE FROM TOP LEFT *Among the enviable collection of antique faience at the Abbaye Saint-André are these rare pieces of 18th-century faience from Apt, a graceful "beggar's purse" and a pair of decorative hounds; the workmanship on even a very small piece from the Faucon atelier is unique and mesmerizing, as this little covered pot adorned with birds, garlands, dancers, and a cherub testifies; blue-and-white mixed-clay faience is a relatively new addition to the Faucon line; before firing, an elaborately worked soup tureen at the Atelier Jean Faucon in Apt exhibits the exquisite detailing that distinguishes each piece; firing turns the trim creamy white and brings out the beautiful colors of the mixed clays.* OPPOSITE *A precisely stacked assortment of Faucon faience cools in the kiln after firing.*

The technique is time-consuming, and Jean, who worked alone or with one assistant in his tranquil atelier, offered only a limited, highly sought-after production. The plaster molds used for the plates were created from an archive of two hundred 18th-century molds dating back to 1730. Sadly, Jean Faucon died too young, in the autumn of 2001. But the tradition of the Atelier Bernard continues in the capable hands of Jean's brother Pierre and Jean's fiancée, Nathalie Savalli. Each new piece created today is not only a tribute to the dedication and passion of Jean and his grandfather, but a testament to the talent that runs deep in the family.

Just east from Apt, along the national route 100, another fine *faiencier*, Antony Pitot, works quietly away in the adjoining grange of his rustic 18th-century farmhouse, creating refined and elegant tableware. Pitot works in the venerable tradition of the region's highly skilled 18th-century potters, using period-inspired molds to produce a dazzling line of mustard-yellow and emerald-green faience with lead-free glazes. In his exquisite collection are graceful pitchers, elegant tureens, and a wide variety of interestingly shaped plates, some round, some leaf-shaped, others octagonal or square. Pitot sculpts by hand the artful décors—fruits, vegetables, the occasional little serpent—that adorn some platters and tureens. The sleek, simple patterns look contemporary but are informed by 18th-century styles, and are produced by Pitot with awesome finesse.

RIGHT Potter Antony Pitot holds a stack of his wares outside his farmhouse atelier in the village of Goult. OPPOSITE The inspiration is from the 18th century, but the dazzling glazes and masterly execution of Pitot's elegant faience, including plates and platters imprinted with vine leaves and other flora, is completely contemporary.

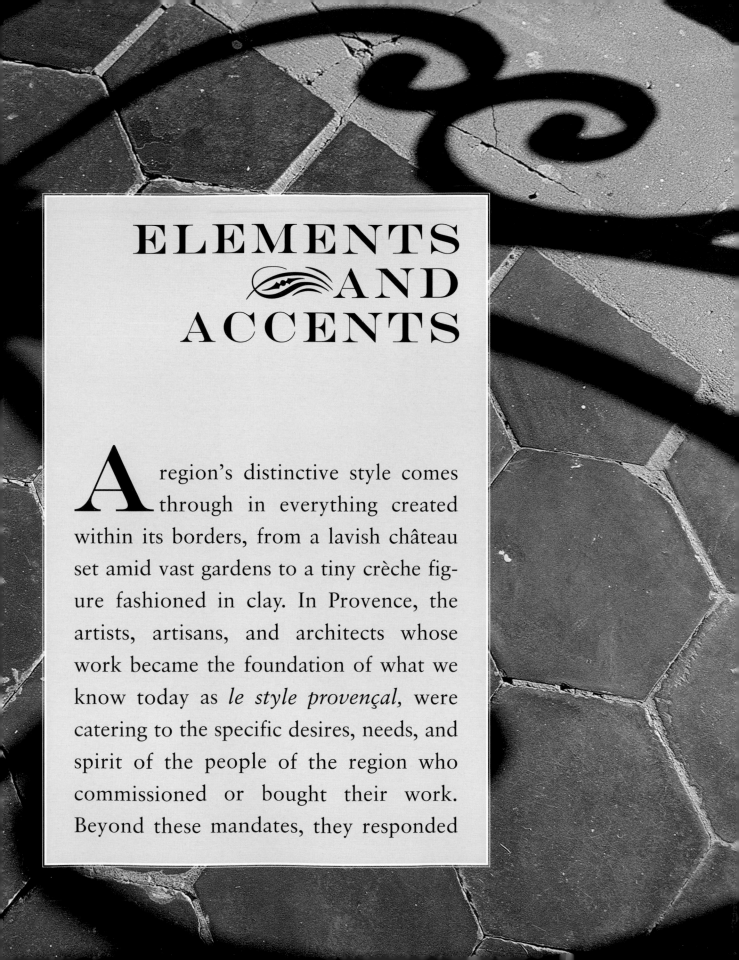

ELEMENTS AND ACCENTS

Aregion's distinctive style comes through in everything created within its borders, from a lavish château set amid vast gardens to a tiny crèche figure fashioned in clay. In Provence, the artists, artisans, and architects whose work became the foundation of what we know today as *le style provençal*, were catering to the specific desires, needs, and spirit of the people of the region who commissioned or bought their work. Beyond these mandates, they responded

to the climate, the sun and the wind in particular; to the gentle influences of other cultures such as Italy, Spain, and the Far East, whose craftsmen or goods made their way into Provence; and to the design trends in Paris, albeit with a delay often of years. The inspired artisans worked exclusively with local, raw materials—wood, stone, clay—which eventually endowed the objects created with a distinct regional harmony.

The architectural details, the decorative accents, and the regional crafts are Provençal elements that, when viewed as an ensemble, have the grace and coherence of a structured style. Used individually, blended into other décors, or as part of a total French Country look,

CLOCKWISE FROM TOP LEFT *Majestic stone medallions separate windows on the upper stories of the 17th-century Hotel La Mirande in Avignon; a study in rectangles, a little window becomes more prominent with a white-painted stone border and a single, weathered-green shutter; a triple-tiered génoise (roof support) crowns the small top-floor window of a village home in the Alpilles; twin white-framed windows in Roussillon assert their individuality with their colors, which holds true for the two-family building's facade.* OPPOSITE, CLOCKWISE FROM TOP LEFT *Contemporary louvered shutters flank a gently arched window just below a stone-framed aperture, now sealed, which was once an attic window; rustic shutters reinforced with iron studs protect a village home in the Vaucluse from the midday sun; porte-fenêtres (French doors) in Avignon open onto a lacy wrought-iron balcony; pillows air out in a square window set into the rustic pierre-sèche (dry-stone wall) facade of the Mas de la Beaume in Gordes.*

these distinctive components lend vivid character to their surroundings. In this chapter, we survey the essential elements and accents that comprise *le style provençal,* from doors and windows, fireplaces, and fountains to wood-beaded curtains, tiles, and tiny sculpted *objets.* Some are antique and some, innovative and fresh, are new. Today's artists, architects, and artisans continue working in the time-honored Provençal tradition, while bringing a contemporary perspective to their work.

Provence's powerful sun and staggering winds have long dictated the size, shape, and position of a regional home's **doors and windows.** To counter the brilliant sun and summertime heat, architects were very fond of a small, round window called an *oeil-de-boeuf* (bull's-eye window). These tiny, circular traditional apertures, often protected by cast- or wrought-iron grills, allowed in refreshing currents of air and perhaps a shaft of light during the heat of the day. *Oeil-de-boeuf* windows were often used on the northern side of a house, which typically was an almost completely closed face, devoid of other apertures, because it was always the colder, wind-battered facade. They were also used high up

ABOVE AND BELOW LEFT *Handsomely sculpted mascarons (stylized masklike faces) adorn the 17th-century limestone-framed windows of Avignon's Hotel La Mirande.* ABOVE RIGHT *A single, spiky wrought-iron guard protects a small window in a 17th-century farmhouse in the Vaucluse.*

on the front facade, just under the eaves, to illuminate an attic room or servant's quarters.

Bastides, châteaux, *maisons de maîtres,* and recent restorations of old farmhouses are enhanced by *portes-fenêtres,* what we call French doors—elongated windows of mullioned glass that open out onto a balcony or terrace. These elegant, tall windows, which are opened to allow in the soft light and air of early morning and cool, lavender-hued evenings, are usually hidden behind long, vividly hued shutters during the heat and light of midday. Some of the best examples of *portes-fenêtres* still have their original bubble-glass, crafted more than a century ago in Biot.

Small, symmetrical carved blocks of local limestone often border and artfully reinforce doors and windows, particularly those that arch. The stone can be very simply finished, or ornately carved and sculpted. Some elegant doorways have lintels adorned with a dramatic carved face, called a *mascaron* (stylized mask). More modest rural dwellings have doorways bordered in wood. While the stone or mortar of a house's facade is often left natural—especially if it is fashioned from the region's beautiful golden-hued limestone—color is frequently used with great zest to trim doors, shutters, and window casements. Blues, greens, red-ochers, sometimes even a grayed lavender embellish shutters and doors, for example, while a window casement might be entirely framed by a heavy border of white paint.

The main door of a Provençal home is typically the focal point of the facade. Doors in the region can be rustic and humble, appropriate for a tiny rural cottage, but they can also be strikingly handsome, massive and heavy, embellished with molded panels, iron studs, or other ironwork trim. Provençal architects and designers have always believed that a great door adds a generous dose of character—and security—to a dwelling. Beautiful antique doors are in high demand at architectural salvage firms such as Jean Chabaud in Gargas, near Apt, and Mille et Une Portes in Carcès.

Many doorways, particularly in southern Provence, where shade is at a minimum during the long days of summer, are covered by **trellises**

CLOCKWISE FROM TOP LEFT *An elegantly paneled Turkish-red door is the striking focal point for a pale pink village home near Gordes; a stately door with recessed panels opens into the Mas de Peint, owned by Lucille and Jacques Bon in Le Sambuc; home today to writer Nicole Cappeau, the 13th-century Monastère du Four, with its vaulted ceilings and massive arched doors built in the hills near Avignon, was once a Benedictine abbey; ornate, slightly Gothic paneling distinguishes the imposing door of a grand* bastide; *a delicate wrought-iron doorpull opens a vintage garden gate in the Alpilles.* OPPOSITE, CLOCKWISE FROM TOP LEFT *A wash of pale blue paint enlivens the 18th-century door of a somber stone home in the Luberon; wrought-iron and cast-iron accoutrements embellish this sumptuous walnut door with Louis XV–style molding in a village home in the Var; a lacy wrought-iron grill protects the window of a farmhouse door near Saint-Rémy; at the Mas de la Beaume, just outside the walls of Gordes, a muslin curtain, dyed a rich persimmon, lets in air and filtered light on a hot summer day.*

lushly blanketed by grapevines or other leafy vines. Also embellishing many doorways, and giving a distinctly characteristic look to Provençal farmhouses and cottages, is a *rideau aux buis* (wood-beaded curtain). This hand-beaded curtain allows for the free flow of air through an open doorway while it blocks the sunlight and offers privacy, permitting people inside to see out, but not the reverse. The curtain also helps to keep the ubiquitous flies of summer outside. Artisans who fashion these curtains have dwindled to less than a handful in France. One of the best is Marie-Claude Brochet, who works alone stringing boxwood beads for custom orders in the atelier inherited from her grandfather south of Avignon. Other, more

ABOVE RIGHT Rideaux aux buis (door coverings strung from boxwood beads), adorn many Provençal doorways, such as this one in Montfavet, at the home of Marie-Claude Brochet, an artisan specializing in these traditional beaded curtains. BELOW RIGHT *An array of patterned wood-beaded curtains greets customers in Marie-Claude Brochet's atelier, where each curtain is custom-made.*

contemporary homes use sheer muslin curtains for the same purpose.

As you drive through the Provençal countryside, you will frequently see small, round columnar structures topped by a tile roof, or extensions adjoining the side wall of a farmhouse or barn that are pierced with small arched holes. These are the region's distinctive dovecotes, called *pigeonniers* or *colombiers*. Once linked to local law and custom, *pigeonniers* were trappings of wealth or prestige, and landowners were once taxed, in part, according to the size of their pigeon population. These days, keeping pigeons is mainly a decorative hobby. The *pigeonniers* were designed with holes—sometimes in the shape of hearts of

clover leaves—just large enough for the pigeons, but too small for birds of prey, such as eagles. *Pigeonniers,* whose interiors can contain hundreds of individual pigeon roosts, range from simple structures, no more than a pyramid of holes cut into the wall under the roof of a barn or church steeple, to architecturally unique, independent structures. Many *pigeonniers* are clad in glazed tiles below the holes, creating a colorful, slippery surface that deters squirrels and other rodents from making their way up and into the shelter.

One of the most beautiful and striking elements in all of Provence's style vernacular is the mottled **terra-cotta-tile roof.** The roofs, produced from sensuously rounded canal tiles, are pitched at a gentle angle, usually 28 to 33 degrees, just steep enough to drain the region's typically light rainfall from the roof, yet without offering major wind resistance to the brutal mistral. The tiles, produced in local clay towns such as Aubagne, Moustiers, Apt, Biot, and Vallauris, come out of the kiln in tones of tan sand, dusty rose, brick red, and tawny brown—depending on the color of the clay, the length of baking, and the tiles' positions in the kiln—and their unpremeditated assembly atop the house

ABOVE LEFT An elegant cylindrical pigeonnier (dovecote) with a distinctive canal-tile roof, commands a corner of an estate garden near Grasse. **ABOVE RIGHT** *Architects had pigeons, as well as more earthbound clients, in mind when they designed this steeple rising above an old stone priory in the Vaucluse.*

CLOCKWISE FROM TOP LEFT *Terra-cotta canal tiles, originally molded— according to apocryphal history—on the thighs of young women, form the beautifully mottled, mosaic-like rooftops of Provence, such as this one in the Luberon; a modest, recently laid double génoise (recessed tiers of tiles) separates the roof from the restored stone walls of a small* mas *in the Luberon; a terraced rooftop shelters sections of a large farmhouse near Bonnieux that was built over several generations.* OPPOSITE *A triple-tiered* génoise *not only supports the roof but adds great visual impact to a home near Ménèrbes.*

gives the Provençal rooftop its distinctive subtly shaded mosaic look.

Sandwiched between the roof and the exterior walls of the house is the classic *génoise,* one of the most characteristic exterior elements of Provençal architecture. The *génoise* comprises from one to four—or, rarely, five—recessed tiers of canal tiles, and serves to link the roof and the exterior wall, protecting both from forceful winds. It also disperses

the weight of the roof evenly over the supporting walls, and extends the roofline so that rain drains directly to the ground without dripping on a house's exterior walls. The tiles and mortar comprising the *génoise*—the name is derived from Genoese, or Genoa-style, implying an Italian influence—are usually left plain, although they may be painted to match the exterior walls of the house.

In restored homes throughout the French countryside, it is fashionable to expose the massive, hand-hewn beams of pine, oak, or sometimes cypress that support the roof, ceiling, and upper floors. The **exposed-beam ceiling** testifies to the age, and age-old craftsmanship, of the house, and imbues the rooms with rugged charm. But displaying structural beams is a fairly recent phenomenon in fashionable homes. In earlier centuries, the exposed beams were deemed "too peasant" by the well-to-do and also were thought of as a fire hazard. Beams and all exposed wood on the walls were slathered with a heavy coat of mortar or plaster.

The **slatted ceiling,** or coffered ceiling, once found mainly in very rural houses, is another once-rustic design element that has enjoyed a remarkable spike in popularity in recent years. Slatted ceilings have been used in many restorations over the last two decades to add an air of rustic elegance and visual allure. The space between the narrowly laid wooden slats is filled in with plaster (or straw and mortar in the old days), giving the ceiling its interesting striped appeal, with the bold stained slats juxtaposed with the softly hued plaster. The exposed slats, called *rondins* in French, serve as supports for the floor above.

In graceful collaboration with the distinctive ceilings within regional dwellings, **tile floors** and **decorative tile work** do much to enhance the appearance of the Provençal interior. Floors are primarily of tile—either glazed or unglazed terra-cotta—for the simple reason that clay was and is more abundant than wood in Provence, and the Provençaux, like most of their compatriots throughout the countryside of France, are thrifty. Provençal *tuileries* (tileworks) created tiles in a variety of shapes and sizes, the most distinctive of which is the hexagonal *tomette,* which first appeared in the 18th century. There are also large and small

squares and rectangles, laid in pleasing geometric patterns, sometimes interspersed with very small contrasting glazed diamond-shaped tiles, called *losanges,* what tile firms in the United States refer to simply as "dots." Easy to clean, cool in the summer, and heat-retaining during the winter, terra-cotta tiles are practical as well as economical.

Other types of tile flooring can be found in Provence. There are marble floors, sometimes laid in intricate trompe l'oeil patterns, but these

ABOVE *A coffered ceiling—its wooden slats stained dark to heighten the visual contrast with the reinforcing mortar—adds a dramatic accent to the dining room of a carefully restored farmhouse in the Luberon.*

ABOVE LEFT *Hand-hewn 18th-century stone tiles pave an orangerie near Nîmes.* ABOVE RIGHT *With care and several centuries of foot traffic, 18th-century terra-cotta tiles develop an incomparable patina.* BELOW *Colorful, late-19th-century cement tiles, like these originals, are returning to vogue, with fine reproductions produced by the venerable Carocim tileworks in Puyricard.* OPPOSITE, CLOCKWISE FROM TOP LEFT *Vintage terra-cotta tiles laid in a random mosaic vary in hue from golden to rose depending upon the blend of clays and their position in the kiln when they are fired; vintage cement tiles harmonize gracefully with 18th-century print wallpaper at the Hotel La Mirande in Avignon; 18th-century tomettes (hexagonal terra-cotta tiles), such as those in this floor, are highly sought after by architectural salvage firms such as Jean Chabaud in Apt; a bright mosaic of 19th-century cement tiles welcomes guests to the Clos des Saumanes, a bed-and-breakfast south of Avignon.*

are reserved almost exclusively to châteaux and other grand aristocratic abodes constructed in the late 17th and early 18th centuries, such as the lavish Château de Barbentane, a château-museum near Avignon. Often, in the entrance halls of upper-class residences, a floor will be composed of large, smooth, elegant limestone tiles, chosen to match the limestone risers and steps of a grand staircase. Finally, in a charming turn-of-the-century home, the eye may be caught by brightly hued cement tiles in solid colors or patterns, usually with a matte finish. Practical and extremely durable, these distinctive tiles, which were in vogue in the late 19th and early 20th centuries, continue to be produced today at the Carocim tileworks in Puyricard, near Aix-en-Provence.

Decorative tilework on kitchen counters, walls, stair-risers, tables, and fireplace extensions called hobs or *potagers,* work harmoniously with tile floors to create a warm and welcoming Provençal ambiance. Beautiful tiles in striking jewel tones are made by a number of artisans, many in the tile village of Salernes. In Apt, Brigitte Benoît-Vernin perpetuates a venerable family business creating handmade, hand-painted, and hand-glazed tiles in a glorious panoply of colors and interesting designs. Old glazed tiles dating back more than two hundred years are often more highly sought after than new ones by architects restoring a period home, or by homeowners looking to enhance a simple fireplace with an intriguing frame of vintage tiles. If the tiles are in fine condition, and some are, all the better; but even cracked or chipped tiles add character and a sense of *temps perdu* to a room.

Hearth and heart have an appropriate similarity in English when it comes to describing the psychic center of the old-fashioned country home. The hearth—the fireplace—was the heart of the house. The similarity does not extend to the French language, but the fact and image of the hearth as the heart of the home remains as true in the French countryside as it is almost everywhere in the world. The **fireplace** (*la cheminée*) in the rural Provençal home was the main source of heat as well as the cooking center. The hearth was equipped with storage niches for condiments, hooks for utensils and hanging pots, large andirons, and a roasting spit. Flanking some rustic fireplaces in an adjacent alcove

OPPOSITE, CLOCKWISE FROM TOP LEFT A wall of multicolored glazed square tiles by Alain Vagh laid in a harlequin pattern borders the pool of an estate near Bonnieux; at the Mas de Peint in the Camargue, blue-and-white hand-painted tiles by Carreaux des Desvres give a lift to the risers of stairs leading to the first-floor bedrooms; these alternating emerald and gold squares by Alain Vagh in Salernes combine to form a backsplash that brightens the kitchen of a Luberon mas; a mosaic of hand-cut jewel-toned glazed tiles is among the most popular patterns at Vernin, Carreaux d'Apt.

is a tile-clad hob, where soups and stews could slowly simmer over glowing embers enclosed below. *La cheminée* was the source of food and warmth, and thus security and well-being.

In an antique home, each fireplace was commissioned for a particular space, so no two are alike. Sometimes they were raised up off the floor a foot or even two, originally to facilitate cooking. Depending on a family's finances, the utilitarian fireplace could be simply chiseled or quite imaginatively carved. Some fireplaces are made of plaster with simple moldings and rounded forms. Others, in bourgeois or aristocratic homes, are of limestone or wonderful local marble, such as the deep rose marble from Brignoles or the mottled gray marble from Cévénol. Elegant renditions might have gracefully bowed uprights in the Louis XV style, and might be carved with a motif of flowers or a cockleshell. Occasionally a sumptuous mantel may be paired with a matching overmantel piece

that makes the *cheminée* even more imposing. In some rustic old farm-houses or ranches in the Camargue, there are enormous fireplaces that are literally cooking alcoves, easily the height of a man, several yards long and many feet deep. Running across the opening of a large rustic fireplace, just under the mantel, is often a small curtain in a bright Provençal cotton print designed to trap the smoke and guide it up the chimney and out of the room.

Staircases in the Provençal home can be either simple or grand affairs, depending upon the character and style of the home. The cardinal rule, and this holds true for any house, is that the staircase is always in proportion to a house and its rooms. In Provence, staircases are often limestone or terra-cotta tiles bordered by wood noses and surrounds, often in oak. Handrails following up the stairway might be carved in stone, worked in graceful wrought iron, or fashioned in cast iron with a smooth wooden rail. Another variation on the handrail is actually a short plaster wall at the staircase's outside edge, which rises to the height of a railing and ends in a sleek molded banister. In many *bastides,* a wide marble stairway rises from the ground floor up to the first story, but from there on up stairways often become more modest, fashioned in tile and wood. In smaller homes, some interior stairways are very narrow gauge, their dimensions adapted to a small corner or

◠OVERLEAF, LEFT In this 13th-century fortress in Joucas known as La Commanderie, a former ruin acquired and superbly restored by international decorator Dan Kiener, a dramatic stone stairway, discovered at an architectural salvage depot, winds its way up to the second floor, where a small window piercing the wall illuminates the passage. OVERLEAF RIGHT Bordered by a cast-iron railing, a graceful stairway à l'escargot mounts to the upper floors; note that stairs from the ground floor to the second floor landing are of hand-hewn stone, while those from the second floor upward—out of view of visitors—are more modestly crafted of wood.◠

hallway or a "stack" of rooms, each on a slightly different level. One of the most beautiful small stairway designs is the handcrafted spiral stairway, called *à l'escargot*.

A lovely, gurgling moss-covered **fountain** evokes many delights at once in Provence: it is both pleasing to the eye and music for the ear. Its perpetually replenished water cools a hot brow, and, for many years if not today, it quenched the thirst of many parched passersby. In some rural villages, fountains, in addition to providing drinking water for the inhabitants, also served as troughs for horses and wash-basins for the village housewives. Water is life in Provence, and the fountain is a captivating and lovely symbol of life. Fountains come in all shapes and sizes in the region, dotting village squares, installed under a group of shady plane trees, or adorning the front garden of a large residential property. The fountain can be as simple as a single spouting orifice above a stone basin, or as elaborate as a tall, moss-covered waterfall topped by a stone or bronze statue. Some of the most intriguing are decorated with handsomely sculpted heads or stylized grotesques called *mascarons,* from whose mouths the water spouts.

Beguiling, imaginative, and expertly crafted **stonework** in many forms is another appealing element of Provençal style. Beyond fountains and fireplaces, lintels and staircases, skilled stonemasons crafted all manner of sculptures for use either indoors or out in the garden. The masons profited from the techniques learned from itinerant Italian sculptors working their way through Provence from the 17th to 19th

LEFT The focal point of a village fountain in the Bouches-du-Rhône is this dramatic cast-bronze mascaron, the head, draped with a lion skin, tinged with verdigris, the beard and paws whitened by the water's chalky lime deposits. OPPPOSITE, CLOCKWISE FROM TOP LEFT *While not always the original intention of the sculptor, the mouth of a stone mascaron often ends up holding the spout of a small fountain; after many years, moss eventually encrusts the stonework of an active fountain, such as this turn-of-the-century village fountain in the Var, whose shower of droplets through the moss form a delicate liquid veil; a grand 19th-century fountain with entwined dolphins, a figure of Neptune, and, of course, a dense layer of moss, greets visitors to Château La Canorgue, a renowned wine-producing estate in Bonnieux.*

centuries. Working in sandstone, limestone, or occasionally marble, the artisans crafted romantic and allegorical sculptures, fruit or floral baskets, and sometimes, pre-1789, religious figures (religious iconography was banned after the Revolution). Another popular subject, which can be often seen on fountains or decorating a house or building facade, were the *mascaron* faces, some of which were whimsical interpretations of the huffing and puffing mistral.

The elegant **wrought-iron** balconies that embellish the cream, ocher, or pink facades of a handsome *bastide* with dramatically contrasting dark detailing are just one example of the Provençal *ferronniers'* (blacksmiths') skilled craftsmanship that accent the homes of the Midi. Imposing wrought-iron gates, sinuous handrails, and garden tables crafted with elegant simplicity are several others. The *ferronniers* of Aix-en-Provence, Carpentras, Arles, Toulon, Uzès, and Nîmes, inspired and taught in the 17th and 18th centuries by Spanish ironworkers, raised ironwork to a high art in the region, and it is a tradition that continues to this day. The strength of the material and the delicacy and grace with which it can be worked has always had a distinct appeal to the Provençal aesthetic. The lines of the ironwork are generally graceful and fluid, recalling the gentle, sensuous curves of Louis XV–style furniture. In addition, some wrought-iron work is enhanced with motifs similar to those on armoires, buffets, and *panetières,* such as flowers, garlands, and ribbons. Renowned *ferronniers,* such as Jean Ferraud in Sarrians, near Carpentras, produce finely crafted wrought-iron balustrades, railings, and garden furniture forged in the 18th-century tradition.

Many small, charming, handcrafted objects accent rooms throughout the Provençal home, adding character and warmth. Decorative or functional, and often both at the same time, these regional crafts can all be grouped under the umbrella of **objets artisanaux.** A widely diverse group they are indeed, comprising, to give just a few examples, the chunky cubes of olive-oil soap from Marius Fabre in Salon; wooden birdcages; carved olive-wood serving utensils; leather or straw boxes; sturdy wicker baskets from Vallabrègues; antique silver and gold jewelry from Marseille, Grasse, and Nice; hand-dipped altar candles

from the Ciergerie des Pré-montrés in Graveson; rustic, three-point wooden harvest ladders from Tarascon; and *santon* crèche figures. As diverse as these objects appear, there are common threads that link them: a freshness and grace of design, a refined sense of color, and the characteristic harmony of line. At base, of course, is the profound respect throughout the region for the traditional handcrafted item, and the artisanal art de vivre.

The most ubiquitous and beloved of all of Provence's *objets arti-sanaux* are the captivating little crèche figures called *santons* (little saints), which are crafted out of clay hand-pressed into plaster molds, generally one to six inches tall, and then hand-painted. More elaborate

LEFT *Gruff, bemused, serene, or dazed, the faces of the many* mascarons *(masklike stone sculptures) that adorn fountains, fireplaces, and facades throughout Provence are full of personality.*

versions are fashioned like large dolls with articulated arms and legs, sculpted heads, and a costume stitched from Provençal cottons. The *santons* represent all the various characters of a typical village: the fisherman, the baker, the miller, the fishmonger, the farmer and his wife, the priest, the washerwoman, the old man bent into the mistral, the gypsy, the shepherd, the minstrel, the town fool, and of course, the Holy Family and the Three Magi. Some *santonniers* (*santon* makers) also create *santons* representing characters from celebrated Provençal novels, such as the lovers Marius and Janette from the stories of Marcel Pagnol.

For several weeks every year during the Christmas season, begininng on the last Sunday in November and ending December 31, there is a major *santon* holiday market—*La Foire aux Santons*—that takes place along the Allées de Meilhan in Marseille, the birthplace of the *santon*. At

OPPOSITE, CLOCKWISE FROM TOP LEFT The hand-crafted limbs of Mamie Martin's santons *await assembly; Mamie decorates her holiday table with antique* santons; *one of her prizewinning crèche scenes includes this peasant woman, whose clothes are made of antique fabrics; this 19th-century-style "traveling salesman"* santon *stands almost 12 inches high.*

SANTONNIÈRE MAMIE MARTIN

One of the most interesting and honored *santon* makers working in Provence today is Mamie Martin, a master *santonnière* who works alone in her atelier in the little village of Aups, in the Var. Although Mamie produces some small reproductions of 18th-century molded clay *santons,* she is celebrated for her large doll-like *santons,* beautifully garbed in costumes Mamie fashions from bits of antique fabric and lace she finds in local flea markets. Mamie—named a *Meilleur Ouvrier de France,* France's highest honor for a craftsperson—sculpts each beautifully defined and soulful *santon* by hand, then accessorizes each with hand-crafted details, such as a pair of tiny wire spectacles or a cluster of miniature clay water pots. Mamie, who trained as a sculptor, is occasionally commissioned to create a large *santon* in the image of someone's father or husband or grandmother. She works from old photographs, and the likenesses she achieves—from the expression on a face to the tiny brass buttons on a military uniform—are uncanny. These commemorative *santons* are unique and extraordinary special-occasion gifts.

ABOVE Mamie puts the finishing touches on a 19th-century provincial cook.

the first *santon* fair in Marseille in 1803, there were three vendors. Today there are dozens coming to sell their wares from all over Provence. The first *santons* appeared just after the outbreak of the French Revolution in 1789, when churches were shuttered and public displays of faith—such as setting up a Christmas crèche peopled with saints—were banned. Jean-Louis Lagnel, an out-of-work sculptor in Marseille, came up with the idea of creating a crèche that featured everyday village people, peasants, and other simple folk that could not possibly offend Revolutionary sensibilities. Created for private family use, the little figures were an immediate success among Provence's frustrated faithful.

Antique *santons,* such as those created by the Frères Batelier in Marseille in the early 1800s, or by Thérèse Neveu in the early 1900s, are extremely collectible. But new *santons,* from famous makers such as Marcel Carbonel in Marseille, Paul Fouques in Aix-en-Provence, and

CLOCKWISE, FROM TOP LEFT At the Ciergerie des Prémontrés in Graveson, paraffin and beeswax candles have been handmade since 1922, using methods that have changed little since the Middle Ages; though renowned for their long, ecclesiastical tapers, the Ciergerie also creates lines of souvenir candles, such as these in the forms of an Arlésienne, a drummer, and the unique Croix Camarguaise *(a cross that incorporates an anchor and a heart); classic, long white tapers await packaging; while most candles at the Ciergerie are boxed or wrapped in cellophane these days, church tapers and votives are still packaged in the firm's famous violet paper.* OPPOSITE *Floating votives and roses add romance to the 18th-century stone fountain—created for a long-lost château—which graces the dining room of the Hotel Le Saint Paul.*

Castelin-Peirano in Aubagne, are collectible as well. You can find *santons* throughout the year at the ateliers of individual producers, but the best selections are available at the many Christmas *santon* fairs, in addition to that of Marseille, that take place in December in cities such as Aix-en-Provence, Aubagne, Les Baux-de-Provence, and Salon-de-Provence. Many friends of mine add one or two new characters to their *santon* families every year, as I do. I find the little figures completely endearing. In fact, just after finishing work on the original *French Country* twenty years ago, I chose two—a winemaker and a village maiden—to crown my wedding cake.

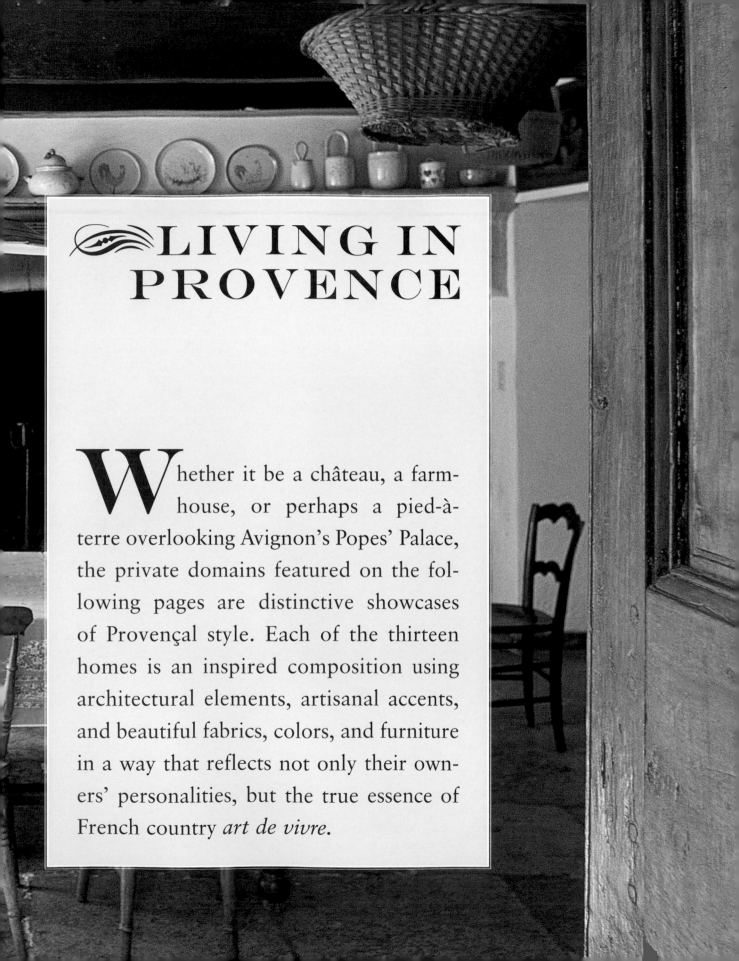

LIVING IN PROVENCE

Whether it be a château, a farm-house, or perhaps a pied-à-terre overlooking Avignon's Popes' Palace, the private domains featured on the following pages are distinctive showcases of Provençal style. Each of the thirteen homes is an inspired composition using architectural elements, artisanal accents, and beautiful fabrics, colors, and furniture in a way that reflects not only their owners' personalities, but the true essence of French country *art de vivre*.

ZEN PROVENÇAL IN THE HEART OF A VILLAGE

ABOVE *A rustic vintage desk in the living room looks out on the intimate enclosed garden.* OPPOSITE *A leaf-shrouded pergola shades the garden's stone-paved path, bordered by a mosaic of small, smooth pebbles. The wrought-iron table and chair are from ASIA in Mollèges, the wicker chair from La Fabrique in Saint-Rémy.*

Secluded behind sturdy wrought-iron gates, the home of three-star-chef Jean-André Charial and his wife, Geneviève, is an intimate oasis in the center of the bustling village of Maussane-les-Alpilles. The house, formerly a storage depot for heating fuel, has been converted with imagination and refinement with the help of architect Alexandre Lafourcade. It provides a welcome sense of privacy and retreat, yet is still just steps away from the village bakeries, post office, and shops. Being close to village life was essential for the Charials, who love doing their errands on foot and having the sense of village life all around them.

Once they acquired their house, their next priority was designing the small, captivating

ABOVE *In her* jardin de curé, *Geneviève Charial, with the help of designer Dominique Lafourcade, created a lovely garden composed of roses, aromatic herbs such as thyme and lavender, and trimmed boxwood.* OPPOSITE *Under a painting by Jean-André Charial's grandmother, an antique console table displays a collection of Christian Tortu vases and a giant sculpted peapod found in Paris.* OVERLEAF *The luminous living room chez Charial reflects the couple's desire for simplicity, with sisal carpets, kilim rugs, and a linen-covered chaise longue. The coffee table is by Michelle Halard; the super-scale urns are from Christian Tortu. The console table was found at a barn sale.*

garden that greets you as you enter through the wrought-iron gates. "We wanted to create a small, very structured garden," recalls Jean-André, "one that would be beautiful all year round, and full of flowers from May through October. We loved the idea of a traditional *jardin de curé,* a curate's garden, which historically was a small garden right next to the vicarage that had a mix of vegetables and flowers." With the help of garden designer Dominique Lafourcade, they conjured a lovely, poetic garden with a vine-covered arbor arching over a stone-paved path. Small, scattered beds with both flowers and aromatic herbs, a groomed lawn shaded by olive and cypress trees, and a pebbled terrace just outside the house complete the design.

The house within reflects a love of Provence blended with a sophisticated modern spirit. A wall of French windows in the spacious living rooms makes the garden, just steps away, almost a decorative presence, along with the comfortable contemporary furniture designed by Michelle and Yves Halard that offered Geneviève the simplicity and soft modern hues that she envisioned. The kitchen, under a ceiling of heavy beams painted pale blue, is streamlined and practical, yet the 18th-century stone fireplace and collections of antique baskets and copper pots—as well as Jean-André's international collection of cookbooks—personalize the sleek, efficient room.

Upstairs, soft, suffused light floods the master bedroom, where a pleasing textural mélange of neutral hues—creams, white, taupe, ivory—is accented by a delicious shock of reds in the bed's beautiful Provençal *piqué* quilt, in the rectangular sofa pillows, and in a lacquered, 19th-century Chinese armoire. The built-in floor-to-ceiling étagère holds books, engravings, and a collection of antique Provençal birdcages. Like the rest of the house, the bedroom is highly edited for comfort and simplicity, evoking a certain Oriental esprit that is the result, perhaps, of the Charials' many voyages to the Far East. In fact, the serenity and elegant restraint chez Charial could be the avant-garde of an intriguing new style, Zen Provençal.

ABOVE *The chef's kitchen is superbly functional and discreetly stylish, without a single* objet *of excess clutter. Linen napkins diffuse overhead lights by Michelle Halard, which illuminate the long rectangular table surrounded by wicker chairs from Belgium.* BELOW *Jean-André Charial's roast fillet of lamb with stuffed tomatoes and braised potatoes awaits guests at Sunday lunch.* OPPOSITE *Garden-fresh ingredients for an early fall lunch brighten the kitchen windowsill.* OVERLEAF, LEFT *The master bedroom is a restful haven of pale neutrals, wih striking raspberry accents in the contemporary Provençal quilt and throw pillows on the sofa. The bed's headboard is an original design by Michelle Halard, the bookcases by Bruno and Alexandre Fourcade.* OVERLEAF, RIGHT *A small antique African carving, posed on a rustic Provençal farm table, surveys his new domain.*

⌒A LAVISH LUBERON FARMHOUSE

⌒ABOVE *An arched stone portal draped in wisteria leads from the garden to the courtyard.* OPPOSITE *Harmonious tones of ocher, cream, and green greet visitors in the entry hall, where a late 18th-century grandfather clock from Avignon stands sentry. The handsome studded door is original to the house.*⌒

"We had traveled and lived in many parts of the world," recounts the dynamic doyenne of this superb estate nestled in the Luberon, "but when we discovered this property with its magnificent view and beautiful old stones, in this gorgeous part of Provence, we fell in love. We knew that this was where we wanted to settle, that this, finally, would be our own piece of paradise."

It took more than three years of dreaming, planning, restoration, and decoration to finally create from this 18th-century property (born in the same year as the French Revolution) a home that fulfilled many dreams. The terraced gardens stretch on to the horizon with groves of olive trees, banks of soaring cypresses to

⊱ABOVE *The cluster of terra-cotta tile roofs testifies to various stages of the property's evolution during the 18th and 19th centuries, with porticos, guest quarters, and a guardian's house added over time.* BELOW LEFT *A majestic allée of cypress trees, flanking an olive grove, leads visitors through the property.* BELOW RIGHT *A variety of antique urns and pots planted with flowers adds touches of brilliant color to the courtyard.* OPPOSITE *A turn-of-the-century country café table and chairs provide an ideal spot for morning coffee while enjoying a panoramic view over the Luberon Valley.* ⊰

buffer the north wind, tennis courts, a swimming pool, a vegetable garden, an herb garden, old fountains, grapevines, fig trees, an antique well, and an open "summer kitchen" with a wood-fired oven. More of a compound than a traditional house, the property, which is enclosed by stone walls, has several smaller buildings, homes for staff, family, and friends, that surround the main house.

The main house is classically structured on a long horizontal plane, with the dramatic addition of a second-floor gallery, or portico, that stretches along the facade, offering dazzling views of the Luberon Valley. Inside, the house showcases the work of many local artisans with handsome displays of tile, stonework, carpentry, cabinetmaking, and wrought iron. For example, a unique wrought-iron banister embellished with sunflowers that was designed by the owners winds up the staircase in the duplex master bedroom. The sunflower is a motif that's repeated on a plaster wall-frieze in the immense, yellow-tiled master bath, equipped with a small, elegant working fireplace and

⌒ABOVE In the heavily beamed kitchen, a floral and trellis composition of tiles form an elegant backsplash for the La Cornue stove. The white and floral tiles are from Delfino in Le Cannet, while the green trellis strips were fashioned by a local mason and then glazed and fired by Vernin/Carreaux d'Apt. BELOW An early-20th-century zinc bar bought (after much persuasion) from a local restaurant, serves as a room divider between the kitchen and dining room. OPPOSITE In the dining room, an unusual early-19th-century buffet-à-deux-corps, painted most likely to conceal its mix of woods, charms with its trompe l'oeil interpretation of Louis XVI design motifs. ⌒

ABOVE The Louis XV banquette provençale *featured on the cover of* Pierre Deux's French Country *inspired the graceful reproduction, custom made for the vaulted living room; lamps rest on vintage folding iron chairs.* BELOW *Two Louis XVI–style* mont-golfier *fauteuils, with hot-air balloon-motif backs, flank an elegant Louis XV Provençal game table.* OPPOSITE *In the master bedroom, a Louis XVI bed, found almost in ruins, was brought back to life with restoration as well as pale green and cream paint.* OVERLEAF *In the dazzling master bathroom, a turn-of-the-century rattan porch chair provides a comfortable place to rest after a bath. The tilework was designed and created by Gilles Delfino in Le Cannet. In the corner, an unusual 19th-century* encoignure *cabinet opens to reveal a three-way mirror and a vanity, an early creation by the Miroiterie Brot.*

a glass-enclosed steam bath. The artisanal touches, along with nostalgic elements from the couples' earlier lives and carefully selected regional antiques, such as a 19th-century Provençal grandfather clock in the entry hall and a turn-of-the-century zinc-top bar from a local restaurant in the living room, make this house not only a poshly comfortable home but a celebration of regional style. The house is a testament to good fortune, good spirits, and the longevity of fine old architecture, and richly merits its name, "Longo Maï," a good wish in old Provençal meaning "Long May It Last!"

A FABRIC FAMILY'S PRIVATE DOMAIN

The limestone facade of the late-18th-century building in an old quarter of Avignon is sober and aloof, giving no hint of the color, patterns, and charm that lie within. Behind the heavy carved door, a wide stone stairway leads to the airy family apartment of Françoise and Jean-François Boudin, owners of the renowned Provençal fabric company Les Olivades. The apartment, with its rich color and multiple patterns, reveals the owners' love for the traditional Provençal fabrics that have been the mainstay of the family for more than a half century. The home is also a template for how these fabrics and patterns can be used abundantly and to great effect, juxtaposed with local tile, stone, and period architectural elements.

ABOVE *In the dining room, an 18th-century wrought-iron and marble console table displays a living still life.* OPPOSITE *The Boudin apartment comprises a floor of a 16th-century mansion. The entrance hall is in tones of flame-red and ocher yellow, "colors that symbolize welcome in Provence," says Françoise Boudin.*

ABOVE *Family heir-looms, the Directoire dining room chairs with painted inset panels of mythological scenes have Les Olivades "Fruchié" pattern cushions covering their rush-woven seats.* OPPOSITE *The dining room walls are also covered in the "Fruchié" pattern (its name means "fruit" in Provençal), a design inspired by an 1829 fabric. Rich with grape bunches, pears, raspberries, cherries, and pineapples, it is per-fect, notes Françoise Boudin, for a dining room. The ornate 18th-century blue-gray marble fireplace is embellished with inlays of red and pink marble; next to the mirror on the right hangs a gilded Directoire barometer.*

Curtains in 18th-century-style red, white, and yellow paisley-printed cotton cover the long windows of the entry hall, in monochromatic harmony with a smaller red print adorning the walls. In the dining room, Les Olivades's merry fruit and flower pattern "Fruchié," here on a ground of saffron yellow, predominates on the walls and chair cushions, while the living room is calm and luminous with walls of white cotton piqué. The romantic master bedroom sets a restful tone with walls of robin's-egg blue and a half-canopy bed that makes sumptuous use of four different blue, white, and rose patterns.

Enhancing the classic regional style are family heirlooms such as the 18th-century walnut commode from Nîmes in the living room, painted Directoire dining-room chairs, and a gilded Regency barometer. The ensemble chez Boudin handsomely encapsulates family traditions, bringing the business home, and making the home a proud reflection of the business in the best of all possible ways.

ABOVE *White and cream tones form the background to the living room, "neutral and restful," notes Françoise Boudin, for a room into which all the other rooms of the house converge. The ornamental moldings, highlighted in white, date from the 18th century. On the green-draped table in the background is an urn-inspired lamp by Paris designer Jean Reverdy.* BELOW *Directoire period doors open onto the sunny kitchen, with yellow and brown wall tiles and terra-cotta* tomettes *floor tiles from Alain Vagh in Salernes.* OPPOSITE *The sumptuous bed treatment in the master bedroom uses three different coordinating Les Olivades fabrics: "Croustado," with garlands and bouquets on the half-canopy's swagged curtains, the headboard, and small pillows; "Naiado," a tiny floral print, on the canopy's lining, the dust ruffle, and large pillows; and "Rayou" in Bastille Red, with stripes and flowers, on the bedspread and the chair. A small 19th-century quilt covers the bedspread.*

AN ANTIQUE MILL IN THE ALPILLES

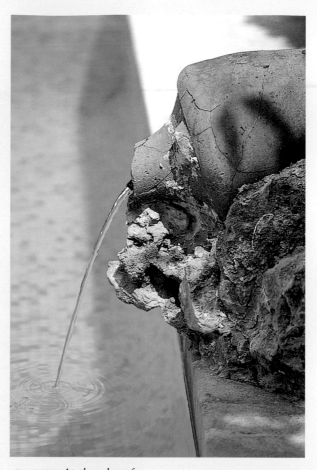

ABOVE *At the edge of the mosaic-tiled swimming pool, a coral- and shell-encrusted terra-cotta urn serves as a unique fountain.* OPPOSITE *The facade is punctuated by a variety of shade trees—including several old mulberry trees—and potted shrubs. A 19th-century park bench sits across from the entrance.*

The bucolic old mill is far away from Paris in many ways, but in travel time the transition is just a few hours thanks to the high-speed TGV train. "I can board the train at five o'clock in Paris, and at eight o'clock I'm in my house, ready for dinner," says the media executive from Paris who bought and renovated the mill several years ago. "This is my 'paradise found.' I came here as a child to visit my grandfather who had an olive-oil mill right next door. Coming back here cures my soul."

Ranks of imposing cypresses, a swath of olive grove, hedges of rosemary, and clusters of brilliant red geraniums surround the Moulin de la Tour, an elegant enclave dominated by an 18th-century former olive-oil mill. The mill,

RIGHT *A wide stone stairway, bordered by towering cypress trees, winds up from the front of the parklike property around to the back.* OPPOSITE *In the dining room, a large, glass-fronted cabinet originally created for a local notary's office today functions as a commodious china cabinet.*

The large round table, draped in a Souleiado quilt, is surrounded by 1930s-style woven chestnut and rattan chairs.

which dates from 1773, was built as a long, rectangular enfilade and has grown horizontally over two centuries. Today this dramatic home with majestic bones is capped by a handsome, triple-*génoise* canal-tile roof. Along one wall, four vaulted niches where the actual olive-oil presses once stood are today semi-private nooks for dining, siestas, and an office. Flanking the vaulted main room are an inviting bullfight-themed bar and billiard room on one end, and the heavily beamed kitchen and spacious pantry on the other.

PRECEDING PAGES *The vast, vaulted central room, comprising the living room and dining room, stretches more than a hundred feet in length, and includes four vaulted niches that once held the mill's olive presses. The walls glow with the golden hues of centuries-old hand-hewn limestone. A vintage Provençal quilt covers the small round table in the foreground. Against the wall between the two niches on the right is one of a pair of rustic 17th-century console tables in walnut.* RIGHT *Just off the vaulted central room is a cozy bar adorned with bull-fighting posters, a sparkling antique toreador's costume, and renderings of bulls' heads in a variety of media, including woven wicker and carved wood. The brass-railed bar came from an old Marseille bistro.* OPPOSITE *Salvaged library shelving has been painted cream and olive and transformed into a kitchen étagère and storage cabinet, displaying vintage Barbotine plates and antique pottery.*

The solidity and golden hue of the mill's antique limestone walls frame the downstairs common rooms, while upstairs the rooms, with lower ceilings and plaster walls, are sponge-painted, two in passionate reds, pinks, and salmons, and one in white and blue. The scale upstairs and down is different as well: downstairs is grand and oversize, dictated by the huge, open main chamber, with big sofas, big tables, big bookcases and cabinets; upstairs is intimate and cozy, with smaller rooms,

lower ceilings, and furniture on a smaller scale. The charming Provençal décor was created with the help of two renowned decorators, the esteemed Provençal designer Estelle Réale and the sought-after Parisienne Marie-José Pommereau. The furniture, a comfortable and eclectic mix of styles and provenance, includes a rustic Louis XVI console table in the living room, a sturdy provincial 1930s desk in the office, and spectacular turn-of-the-century wall-size cabinets from a local dry-goods shop in the dining area. In the kitchen, old library shelving holds glassware and pottery. Accented with softly worn quilts, 1950s-era faience from Vallauris, and bullfighting bric-a-brac, the décor reflects a passion for the deep Midi.

Although just at the edge of a town, the Moulin de la Tour conveys the impression of being deep in the countryside. The house is sur-

ABOVE The contemplative blue bedroom harmoniously combines family portraits with vintage wrought-iron garden furniture, a linen-covered armchair, and an ornate 18th-century console.
OPPOSITE Unusual window treatments embellish the French doors, with Persian-blue linen voile covering—and faintly obscuring—the blue and white Souleiado cotton damask beneath.

RIGHT *The sponge-painted salmon-pink walls with pale olive trim of the master bathroom extend the color scheme of the master bedroom suite. A pair of large square gilt-framed mirrors enhances the natural light from the room's single small window.* OPPOSITE *Curtains of sheer Swiss mousseline fabric drape the master bedroom's romantic and feminine wrought-iron bed, designed by Estelle Réale from old elements; an antique white* boutis *quilt covers the bed.*

rounded by terraced gardens, accessed by broad stone steps banked by pots of geraniums. At the front of the house, an azure pool beckons in one corner of the garden, not far from a six-hundred-year-old olive tree. Along the rear of the house, the traditionally more closed northern facade, a line of boxwood topiary balls stand at attention, like a troop of small sentinels. Beyond them, stretching north, are the olive groves that once supplied the mill.

AN ANTIQUE DEALER'S FARMHOUSE REDEFINED

ABOVE *Affordable treasures await in Catherinee Ligeard's* brocante *shop.* OPPOSITE *A 19th-century* buffet provençal *sits below an 18th-century painted canvas panel. In the foreground is a charming late-18th-century Provençal chair with a cushion stitched from an old quilt.*

Catherine Ligeard's little *brocante* shop in the hillside village of Goult, where she sells modest antiques and collectibles from the late 19th to early 20th century, testifies to her sharp eye and refined taste. Always scouring flea markets and estate sales, she knows quality, charm, and a good deal when she sees it. When hunting for a house in the Luberon with her companion, Gérard Gormier, these skills served her well. She immediately fell in love with a small 18th-century farmhouse in the middle of vineyards and pasture, in spite of the tasteless "mod cons" that had been added over the past fifty years. Linoleum, plastic, and Formica did their best to hide the little house's heart and soul, but not from Catherine.

The couple worked over two years to completely renovate the property, paring the house down to its original bones, then building it up into a luminous, comfortable 21st-century house with the charm of a true antique. They restored the traditional old elements they discovered on the property, among them an early-19th-century stone beehive oven outside the kitchen and, several yards away from the house, buried under a scrubby lawn, an unusual square *aire à battre le blé*—a broad,

stone-cobbled threshing floor where the resident farmer milled his grain in the 1700s. Period architectural elements, such as an 18th-century limestone mantel discovered at a local salvage company, Jean Chabaud, and antique stone surrounds for the window apertures, enhanced the interior and the facade.

Finally, Catherine set to work decorating the house *objet* by *objet,* as she came across things she loved in flea markets throughout Provence. Nothing grand or pretentious, just lovely, unassuming pieces: a rustic painted 19th-century buffet, Baumann bistro chairs, classic Provençal antique quilts called *piqués,* and a rush-seated "nursing chair," perfectly in keeping with the spirit of the original house itself. She kept the palette soft and luminous, mostly white and gray with discreet dashes of cinnabar red. The house, sheltered by a wall of cypress trees from the nearby road that leads to Gordes, is as welcoming and romantic in spirit as Catherine herself.

LEFT *In the romantic master bedroom, sheer embroidered curtains silhouette a low, late-19th-century* chaise de nourrice *(nursing chair).* OPPOSITE *In her vintage kitchen full of culinary collectibles, a strip of antique crocheted fabric forms a small curtain to help guide cooking smoke up the old chimney. Curtains in gray-blue cotton camouflage storage areas on either side of the stove. Atop the chimney mantel are a set of 1920s canisters, and molds.* OVERLEAF, LEFT *In a corner of the master bedroom, a modest 19th-century country desk faces a window curtained with vintage quilts thumbtacked to the wall.* OVERLEAF, RIGHT *Charmed by this young, unknown woman's expression, and the lovely original frame, Catherine hangs her portrait prominently in the upstairs hallway.*

A GRAND BASTIDE NEAR LES BAUX

Like many grand country houses in France, this beautiful *bastide* in the Alpilles has a rich history. Part of the foundations date from the 14th century, when it was a modest retreat for the monks from the nearby Abbaye de Montmajour. By the 17th century the property was in private hands, and over the next two centuries many additions were made, making the house larger and more lavish with each successive touch. It nevertheless remained comparatively austere until the early 1900s, when an American oil baron, an heir to the Standard Oil fortune, bought the property and turned it into a big-money showplace. Stretching from the front of the house, he added Italianate gardens complete with stone muses at every turn,

ABOVE *Recently added French doors bring much-needed light to the old stone kitchen's interior (see pages 144–145).*
OPPOSITE *A wrought-iron gate, crafted for the portal a hundred years ago in a traditional Provençal zigzag pattern, marks the main entrance to the* bastide *and its gardens.*

A manicured wall of arbovitae includes a doorway clipped into the center, giving access from one part of the garden to another; a traditional harvest ladder from Jean-Claude Guigne in Tarascon temporarily blocks a path leading to a tall garden pavilion built in the early 19th century; a Florentine crest emblazoned with a unicorn crowns the lintel above the bastide's *main entrance; in a sheltered niche of the formal French gardens, a pair of stone putti oversee an 18th-century stone garden pool.*

OPPOSITE *The owner's collection of flea-market paintings of regional Provençal landscapes adorns the wall in a corner of the library. An antique kilim covers the table. The chair is a turn-of-the-19th-century reproduction of an 18th-century fauteuil, one of a set that came with the purchase of the house.*⌒

inspired by the famous Boboli gardens behind the Pitti Palace in Florence, and created formal French gardens to the side of the house. The home was the site of many grand balls and garden parties, rare events in the Provençal countryside at the turn of the 20th century. By the end of World War II, the property had reverted to a French family, who in the mid-1980s sold the house and its history to its current owners, a multinational couple with roots in France, both of whom had a passion for Provence.

"We were looking for something unusual, with gardens and a lot of room for family and friends, but still close to a village," recalls the owner. "When we first saw the property, it was in a bad state—neglected, overgrown, a bit depressing. But we fell in love with it and we could see the potential . . . *and* all the work it would require!"

In fact, after a series of amazing coincidences, it seemed like the purchase was virtually preordained. In an old box of family mementos, a sister-in-law discovered postcards of the property, sent to a great-grandmother by a relative who had been a guest at the house in the 1920s. Then, after a recent family wedding at the property, a new in-law said that there was something hauntingly familiar about the house. She went home to Paris and found a small watercolor of the house dated May 27, 1918, painted by the Standard Oil heir himself for the in-law's great-aunt, and handed down through her family.

Over several years, the current owners restored the formal gardens to today's splendor, and room by room renovated the interior. They

ABOVE *In the dining room, a 1940s copy of a Regence table can open to accommodate fourteen. The chairs are 19th-century Regence reproductions covered in vintage fabric. To the right of the window, a cabinet created from a salvaged 18th-century buffet door provides storage. Next to the fire-place is a 19th-century theatrical-prop flowerpot.* OPPOSITE *The library cabinets, installed in the 1930s, are replicas of the library wall in Avignon's Calvet Museum.*

ABOVE A 19th-century sofa covered in a bright cotton jacquard is the focal point of the vaulted living room. Straddling the corner on the right is an 18th-century tapisserie pauvre *(tapestry for the poor)—a canvas wall hanging painted to look like a hand-loomed tapestry.* BELOW *A lavish 18th-century gilt mirror, reflecting a family portrait, hangs above a graceful Louis XV stone fireplace in a guest bedroom.* OPPOSITE *The living room offers views of a lovely 18th-century fruitwood desk, a Louis XIII armchair with needlepoint upholstery, and a Louis XV caned side chair. The large lantern light fixtures were designed by the owners, inspired by a Louis XIV original, and crafted by a local wrought-iron artisan.* OVERLEAF, LEFT *In a guest bedroom, 19th-century beds have been repainted and upholstered with* toile de Jouy. *While adding a romantic touch, the sheer netting actually serves to rebuff mosquitoes.* OVERLEAF, RIGHT *In a second guest bedroom, an 18th-century side chair from Arles rests on* tomettes *tiles from the same period.*

tore up all the red, white, and black tiling downstairs and got rid of the carpeting upstairs, replacing everything with 18th-century stone and terra-cotta, found at an architectural salvage firm. They then stripped several 18th-century fireplaces, buried under heavy coats of gray paint, down to their original marble, and modernized several bathrooms. The house's 18th- and 19th-century provincial furnishings, found at antiques dealers, flea markets, and auctions in France and England, are carefully in keeping with the estate's distinct personality and uniquely storied history. In the home's major renovation, the owners created the big rustic kitchen from the *bastide*'s oldest room, a ground-floor space opening out onto the garden that was previously used as a back bedroom. This large room, with its 14th-century foundation and its 15th-century fireplace and stone-slab floors, was the original monks' retreat, and the owners strove to create a functional family kitchen while maintaining the space's austere, historic beauty.

A ROMANTIC'S "PARROT PERCH"

ABOVE *A small terra-cotta statue of a little boy gazes into a garden pool.* OPPOSITE *In a small salon, Jean-Jacques Bourgeois mixes one of his reproductions—a Louis XVI fauteuil with Pierre Frey fabric on the cushions—with his originals, such as the 18th-century stone fireplace and early 19th-century crèche figures.*

Although it is abundantly clear from even a short visit to his home, Jean-Jacques Bourgeois restates the obvious: "I can't bear modern things!" This well-respected antiques dealer, thirty years in the business in L'Isle-sur-la-Sorgue, lives in the modest 17th-century stone house where both his grandmother and mother were born. Once a *relais de poste,* or post-house where carriage horses were changed on the road south to Marseille, the hillside house was built on a quirky vertical plan, a *"baton du perroquet,"* or a parrot perch, as they say in Provence, meaning a house cobbled together with one room on top of the other. There was an adjoining stable, which is now a bedroom; and a goat house niched in the rocks has been

ABOVE LEFT *In a small garden niche, an 18th-century stone birdbath carved with acanthus leaves offers the many varieties of local birds a chance for a cool dip.* ABOVE RIGHT *In one of several settings for outdoor dining scattered over the property, four 19th-century folding metal garden chairs surround an early-20th-century café table.* OPPOSITE *A large collection of rustic cages, for carrying birds or small animals to market, decorates the walls of the covered terrace where Jean-Jacques's family and friends enjoy dining. The early-20th-century folding chairs once provided seating at a local theater. The wrought-iron chandelier is an 18th-century-style Vincent Mit L'Ane reproduction.*

converted into a bathroom. Over the years, the house has gently expanded horizontally.

Narrow stairways, some *à l'escargot* (spiral), others straight, lead up or down to each intriguing small room. At one point, the home was divided in half, for two branches of the same family to live side by side. In renovating the house, returning it to its original state, and making very few concessions to modern life, Jean-Jacques opened up divided rooms, and in the process made a number of discoveries, such as 18th-century doors hidden under layers of plaster in the walls. Out in the garden, he created several small terraces and carved out shaded garden nooks from the lush greenery. "I love these small, intimate spots scattered over the property," he says, surveying his domain. "They're perfect for dining in different seasons, different moods, different light."

An inveterate collector with a passion for the late 18th and early 19th centuries, Jean-Jacques has filled his home with a trove of period furniture, faience, antique fabrics, and *objets*, juxtaposed with his own reproductions, sold under the Vincent Mit l'Âne sobriquet, also the name of his shop. In a tiny upstairs salon, for example, treasure and reproductions are cheek by jowl: an ornate gilded Louis XIV mirror

tops a Louis XV small stone fireplace, while in front of the fireplace sits a Vincent Mit l'Âne copy of an 18th-century Provençal fauteuil, a rush-seated Jean-Jacques Bourgeois specialty. Everywhere, there are candlesticks and chandeliers for candles. At night Jean-Jacques's house glows with candlelight.

Furniture is perfectly in scale with the small, low-ceilinged rooms, a decorative touch not always easily accomplished. For a small guest bedroom, Jean-Jacques searched ten years before he found chairs with the proper proportions and scale for the room. When he did, he discovered not only graceful needlepoint-covered chairs, but at the same time, a portrait of the 19th-century lady who stitched the needlepoint. Her image graces the wall near the fireplace.

As in almost every traditional French Country family home, furniture spans the centuries as well as regional styles. Each piece of furniture, each *bibelot* and *objet,* has its own story, and Jean-Jacques passionately loves recounting the tales of the antiques that found their way to his home. For this unapologetic romantic, it is not only the thing in itself that beguiles him, but rather the life it has lived, its history, and the sense of its past that contributes eloquently to his present.

ABOVE LEFT *The 17th-century house's original common room is today the dining room. The early-19th-century painted Italian armoire holds a collection of antique faience. The rush-seated dining chairs are Directoire.* ABOVE RIGHT *Along the mantel, early-19th-century faience kitchen pots from Agde alternate with early-20th-century candlesticks.* OPPOSITE *A dazzling 18th-century Provençal silk piqué quilt drapes a table in a small salon that was once the home's entry hall. Above hangs a graceful Directoire chandelier, the same epoque as the rush-seated chairs painted with bucolic landscapes.*

ABOVE *Jean-Jacques transformed a rocky niche that once sheltered a flock of goats into an unusual guest bathroom with cast-cement countertops and rustic accents, such as a 19th-century carpenter's cabinet with drawers and little shelves and an early-20th-century farm stool.* BELOW *A striking red-and-white-striped 19th-century Provençal quilt, laid on the diagonal, brightens a low-ceilinged bedroom where everything has slightly reduced proportions, such as the scaled-down Louis XVI needlepoint-covered fauteuil. Above the chair is a portrait, a serendipitous discovery, of the very lady who stitched the chair's coverings.* OPPOSITE *The décor of a whimsical little bedroom that Jean-Jacques calls "The Niche" is entirely devoted to antique dogs— portraits, toys, statues, even a 19th-century plaster bank, poised on a sturdy Directoire walnut chair. A late 18th-century piqué quilt covers the bed.*

~AN AUSTERE STONE FARMHOUSE WITH A COLORFUL SOUL

~ABOVE *In a sponge-painted French blue guest bedroom, a gilded Napoleon III ciel de lit (half-canopy) with toile hangings adds a theatrical touch.* OPPOSITE *The long upstairs hallway combines the colors—bright yellow, cherry red, French blue— of all the bedrooms that give onto it.*~

From the outside, this handsome 18th-century stone farmhouse in the Alpilles is sober and discreet, with its unadorned weathered stone walls and gunmetal-blue shutters and doors. But the interior reveals a deep passion for lush color, a passion shared by both the current and previous owners, who are friends. The colors brighten the low-ceilinged and often small-scaled rooms. But where the colors were a bit too vibrant, daring, *"très flash"* in the house that the new owner acquired, she sought to soften the tones to her own taste, particularly in the living areas. Today, instead of the vivid yellows and reds that had prevailed throughout the downstairs rooms, there is a palette of rich creams and soft yellows, accented by furniture

ABOVE The gracious 18th-century farmhouse's discreet facade, with its natural stone walls and muted blue shutters, reveals nothing of the exuberant palette that lies within. Unusual among the many area farmhouses is this property's verdant lawn. BELOW The traditional stone bench that typically sits by a mas's kitchen door is here replaced by a vintage park bench. OPPOSITE In a vaulted niche near the living room, two Napoleon III–style chairs, with seats upholstered in a Pierre Frey toile, flank a simple turn-of-the-century garden table. Above hangs a mid-19th-century chandelier originally created to illuminate a church altar.

sporting an array of blue-printed fabric. "I wanted the colors downstairs to be very light and luminous," the owner explains, "to give the impression that the rooms were flooded with sunlight, winter and summer. To harmonize with the soft yellow, I loved the varied blues of the fabrics; they're not only easy to live with but they act as *un fil conducteur*, a unifying thread that ties together the blue of the shutters outside with the blues in the bedrooms."

Upstairs the palette—unchanged from the previous owners—bursts into a brilliant rainbow arcing from red to indigo and including yellow, green, and soft blue in the ensemble of hallways, bedrooms, and bathrooms. In many of the rooms the color was applied with large sponges to give a variation in tones to the walls.

One small bedroom is fuchsia, with a fuchsia-and-white striped upholstered headboard, and sheer chartreuse organdy curtains fall in a

LEFT Oeil-de-boeuf *windows bring light from the rooms into the long, windowless hallway.* RIGHT *An Italian crystal chandelier, purchased on a trip to Rimini, lights up a steep stairway to an adjoining wing of the house.* OPPOSITE, ABOVE *A heavy linen tablecloth covers the Louis XVI dining table, surrounded by a set of chairs discovered at a local flea market.* BELOW *The small vaulted living room is set up for intimate conversation, with two sturdy Louis XV armchairs facing two early-19th-century Provençal fauteuils. A 19th-century canapé Marseillais, (Marseille-style sofa) covered with a nautical toile print from Pierre Frey, provides room for three or four more.* OVERLEAF, LEFT *An ecclesiastical candelabrum blooming with tole-work lilies complements the 19th-century painted firescreen that covers the hearth of an 18th-century fireplace in the yellow guest bedroom.* OVERLEAF, RIGHT *In the red bedroom, chartreuse organdy curtains hanging from a wrought-iron* ciel de lit *add a contrasting note to the room's dominant color.*

soft cascade around the head of the bed from a wrought-iron *ciel de lit* (half canopy). Another bedroom is goldenrod with a deep gold Provençal *piqué* quilt on the bed and sheer organdy curtains in yellow and celadon descending from another *ciel de lit*. A third bedroom is a cozy pastiche of rich blues, and a fourth, set off on its own in another corner of the house, is deep taupe and cream with dramatic Empire-inspired twin wrought-iron bedsteads, and plaid bedspreads in olive, cream, and cherry.

With whimsy and a sure eye for tone, the upstairs hallway unites the cluster of bedrooms giving onto it with a dominant yellow hue accented by cherry red and rich French blue. Helping to illuminate the long narrow hallway are high porthole-like *oeil-de-boeuf* (bull's-eye) windows piercing the walls above doorways to allow light to flow out into the hall while preserving privacy within the rooms. In this house where color is king, furnishings and decoration have been kept simple, with provincial 19th-century furniture, some painted, some stained and upholstered, gilt-framed engravings, and modest 19th-century candelabras and lamps illuminating the cheerful ambiance.

A GALLIC RANCH IN COWBOY COUNTRY

The Camargue is a world apart from anything else in France. Set in the Rhône delta at the southwestern tip of Provence, this broad, flat land by the sea is startling in its luminous intensity. In stark contrast to the rest of Provence, with its olive groves, rolling countryside, and fields of sunflowers and lavender, the topography of the Camargue is filled with pampas-like plains, pastures, rice fields, salt marshes, and sand dunes, much of which today is part of a vast, rigorously protected nature reserve. Populating this distinct and unforgettable realm that revels in its "otherness" are bronzed ranchers, brightly clad cowboys called *gardiens*, gypsies, haunting white horses, pink flamingos (among the four hundred species of birds that

LEFT Chasing away the raseteurs who are trying to grab the pom-pom placed between his haunches, a bull proves who is master of the ring, at the arena in Mouriès. RIGHT *Deep green trim on doors and shutters contrasts starkly with the gleaming white-washed facade typical of many Camarguais ranches.* OPPOSITE *The ranch's office testifies to the property's raison d'être—horses and bulls. One of the owners stud-monogrammed saddles rests in the foreground. Mounted over the desk is the proud head of one of the ranch's prizewinning bulls—Soulléu, who died, like most competitive bulls in the Camargue, of old age; he was 18.* OVERLEAF *The huge 19th-century raised fireplace warms the rustically beamed living room, once a shelter for cowboys and stable hands. Bull trophies won over the decades dominate the décor. The fireplace's alcove potager (hob) once used for cooking soups and stews, now displays collectibles. A vintage Souleiado fabric covers the cushion on the rush-seated banquette.*

flourish here), and, most notably, big black bulls, some of which achieve legendary status in the ever-popular regional bullfights, called *corridas*. In these fiercely contested competitions between man and beast, the bulls—their horns adorned with *cocardes,* or pompoms, that white-garbed, fleet-footed young men called *raseteurs* try to pluck off in the arena—are never killed.

Many of the finest houses in the Camargue are ranches, called *mas* here, the same word used for farmhouses in other parts of Provence. Thick white plaster and stone walls enclose low, modestly proportioned rooms with ceilings of massive, hand-hewn beams and small, widely spaced windows. The design keeps the interiors cool, despite the often pulsating heat outside. When the weather turns chill, enormous old fireplaces, sometimes extending the length of a wall, heat the rooms, warming the stone walls and terra-cotta floors, which retain the warmth for hours.

One of the most handsome *mas* in the Camargue is home to a celebrated local family, noted equestrians and breeders of prize-winning bulls. Dating from 1818, the ranch was acquired in 1944 by the owner's father, who took it on as a shelter for stable hands and *gardiens,* rather than for his own residence. The property's transformation into a "master's house" began in 1964, when the newly married owners moved in

and commenced a long-term restoration. The domain encompasses more than 1,500 acres, ample space to graze their 500-head *manade* (herd) of black bulls, the most famous of which was Goya, a magnificent, wily bull who competed in the local *corridas* for almost two decades before dying of old age in 1986.

The ranch, surrounded by stables, corrals, and pasture, is a striking and harmonious blend of fine heirloom furniture and classic Provençal style with the Wild West trappings of cowboy country: lariats, saddles, broad-brimmed felt hats, and trident-shaped bull prods. Souleiado cotton-print pillows spark the predominantly wood, stone, and leather décor, just as a collection of more than two hundred colorful Souleiado shirts brightens the work clothes of the owners, who ride out daily to the bulls. Brimming with heart and soul, this *mas* exudes great pride in the traditions of old Provence. Singled out for special honors in the pride department, with an abundance of photos, citations, and indeed his mounted head above the desk in the ranch's office, is the celebrated Goya. Intrepid and beloved, Goya, who could leap over an arena's barricades to chase after the *raseteurs* who had the effrontery to attempt to pluck off his *cocardes,* is in fact an iconic bull, immortalized several years ago with his own, bigger-than-life bronze statue in the center of the nearby town of Beaucaire.

ABOVE *A long Louis XV–style dining table accommodates dinner guests under a coffered ceiling. The* armoire de mariage, *with elegant* ferrures, *stores vintage linens.* OPPOSITE *The dining room's lavishly sculpted Arlesien panetière, carved with musical instruments and flowers, and the richly patinaed pétrin beneath, carved with flowers and a soup tureen, are glowing examples of regional craftsmanship.*

A PIED-À-TERRE IN AVIGNON

ABOVE *For a dinner à deux, a Louis XV–style game table is set with an oversize 18th-century linen kitchen towel and early-19th-century plates from Gien, in the Loire Valley.* OPPOSITE *Gertjan van der Hoest found a 19th-century over-mantel mirror that miraculously matched the size and scale of the 19th-century marble mantel.*

For years, Gertjan van der Hoest, a Dutch caterer and antiques dealer from the old town of Briele, near Rotterdam, had dreamed of having his own little place in Provence. Yet it wasn't until he saw the tiny walk-up apartment in the heart of Avignon, steps away from the historic Palais des Papes, the Popes' Palace, that he knew he had found the dwelling that suited his needs perfectly. Suggested to him by Avignon friends, the apartment, part of a grand 17th-century house, was originally added in the late 19th century as *chambres de bonnes* (maids' rooms).

Two small bedrooms, a small living room, and a long galley kitchen were all Gertjan van der Hoest needed for his modest foothold in

Provence. The apartment was without character or detail, not surprising for former servants' quarters, but Gertjan changed all that with a few savvy renovations, a restrained olive-and-cream color scheme, and carefully chosen antiques. A large 19th-century Louis XV–style mirror exactly matching the width of the small marble mantel added light and depth to the small living room. A few good paintings, such as a gilt-framed 1750 portrait of a mistress of Louis XV, give the room character and a touch of richness.

Gertjan transformed the narrow kitchen, with the help of an Avignon cabinetmaker, into a marvel of elegant simplicity and practicality, with a long countertop of Carrara marble topped by graceful open shelving painted soft gray-blue. The apartment's one splash of bright color appears in the master bedroom, in the 19th-century sleigh bed's scarlet coverlet and pillows. The apartment's most dramatic feature, and the deal-clincher when Gertjan visited for the first time, lies just outside the window: a breathtaking view from both bedrooms of the Palais des Papes' majestic stone walls.

CHÂTEAU DE L'ANGE

ABOVE *The namesake of the château, a chubby 18th-century angel crowns the fountain in the Mézard courtyard.* OPPOSITE *Angels appear throughout the house, as they do here in a slightly battered vintage canvas. The golden wooden arrow caught Edith's fancy at Michel Biehn's shop in Isle-sur-la-Sorgue.*

The setting is less than completely tranquil as this château is tucked behind tall iron gates just off the busy main street of Lumières, a small hamlet in the Luberon. But the graceful 18th-century Château de l'Ange is full of heavenly light, lavish linens, and a varied array of little angels, the recurring theme of the château. Home to Edith Mézard, creator of exquisite hand-embroidered linens prized all around the world, the château adjoins an airy white atelier where Edith and a small team of expert embroiderers work stitch by stitch to create the sought-after wares for bed and table. Below the atelier, giving onto the heavily shaded courtyard, is the small shop where Edith's most recent collections are sold.

CLOKWISE FROM TOP
LEFT *The rear of the
château overlooks a rec-
tangular reflecting pool
bordered by shrubs and tall
cypresses; the park-like
gardens require daily main-
tenance; the angel's 18th-
century fountain is the
centerpiece of the château's
courtyard.* OPPOSITE *In the
kitchen, Edith's house-
keeper and talented cook
prepares a creamy cherry
clafoutis for lunch. The
wicker baskets, custom
woven for the space,
hold utensils.*

Looking for a home for herself, her husband, and her three sons and
a workshop and boutique for her linens, Edith found the virtually
derelict château in 1990 and began renovating the building and its gardens. In honor of the enchanting stone cherub balancing in the center
of the courtyard fountain, she named the property "Château de
l'Ange," château of the angel.

While the walls of the winding staircase in the entry hall are the

deep terra-cotta red of the nearby Roussillon hills, a vintage hue Edith left as she found it, most of the interior is washed in a matte white, which enhances the ephemeral white voile curtains hanging from the tall French windows. Floating above the hem of each curtain are gracefully embroidered lines of text from beloved Provençal writers, such as Alphonse Daudet, Jean Giono, Frédéric Mistral, and René Char. *"Quand les mystères sont très malins,"* reads one elegantly stitched line by Jean Giono, *"ils se cachent dans la lumière."* "When little secrets are very clever, they hide themselves in the light."

Furnishings in the airy, luminous rooms are elegant and simple, with Edith's prized pieces of Provençal furniture, such as the 18th-century walnut *buffet-à-glissants* in the dining room, juxtaposed with contemporary designs by Jacqueline Morabito and Hervé Baume. Throughout, from kitchen to living room to bedroom, color is minimal, while sculptural form, fine detail, and texture—crisp linen, nubby woven straw, sheer voile—are paramount. Edith's palette, at home as well as in her work, is resolutely neutral, with no vivid hues—apart from the entry hall—in evidence. "I consider whites, grays, and beige as colors, and not the absence of color," she says, "and I really love them, the same way I really love tea with lemon, Italian cuisine, and embroidery. But my preferences of color are just for me personally. I adore vivid colors in other peoples' homes."

Two motifs predominate in the prized collections that accent many rooms chez Mézard. One, of course, is the angels, antique and new, offered over the years by many friends. The other is the "Arlésiennes," the traditionally costumed, raven-haired young women of Arles, widely reputed for their beauty. The Arlésiennes were immortalized in the

LEFT *A covey of* Arlésienne *santons, garbed in "Edith-hued" costumes of white, beige, and pale gray, stand poised on a living room shelf designed by Jacqueline Morabito.* OPPOSITE *In the dining room, a handsome 18th-century* buffet-à-glissants, *a family heirloom sculpted with olive branches and wheat, forms a backdrop for lunchtime's cooling cherry clafoutis. To the left is one of Edith's hand-embroidered monogrammed linen napkins.* OVERLEAF *Edith Mézard natural linens cover the comfortable contemporary sofas and armchairs that make the living room so inviting. The striking early-20th-century cast-bronze figurine on the table at the right depicts Miréo, or Mireille, the tragic heroine of one of Frédéric Mistral's epic poems.*

ABOVE *In the master bedroom, where a blue-and-white-tiled hearth warms the room, two unusual, late-19th-century pieces of furniture—a side table and an elaborate chest-on-chest—are fashioned from wooden thread bobbins.*
BELOW *The bedroom is a major repository for Edith's angel-motif antiques.*
OPPOSITE *Impeccably embroidered, the sheer voile curtains allow soft-focus views of the gardens.*

works of Léo Lélée, an early-20th-century Provençal artist, whose drawings and original posters adorn the white walls of the Château de l'Ange. The Arlésiennes are also popular subjects for local *santonniers*, makers of Provence's traditional clay crèche figures, and eight particularly lovely dancing Arlésienne *santons*—costumed in white and gray—are poised in mid-farandole on a long wooden shelf in the living room.

Passionately Provençal, Edith, born a few miles away in Cavaillon, where her grandmother taught her the art of embroidery, pays homage to her region in a fresh and contemporary way that is totally her own.

Quand les mystères sont très malins ils se cachent dans la lumière.

Jean Giono.

A DECORATOR'S VIBRANT DOMAIN

When Nono Girard's friends seek the words to describe her striking home in Carpentras, they usually revert to the same phrase: *"C'est très Nono!"* It's very Nono. A long-time decorator whose work embellishes both houses and hotels throughout Provence, Nono, a true Provençale, born in Cavaillon, is known for her love of color and lavish detail.

Color, in fact, brings out the poetry in Nono's soul: "It's surely because the Provençal sky is so perfectly blue that I use so little of this color in decorating," she says. "But how can I resist the reds—poppy red, blood red, madder red, cherry, tomato? Or the yellows of the sunflowers, the sun, lemons, mimosa, the soft yellow of ripe wheat? Or even the greens, from

ABOVE *A 1930s bull's head that once graced a local butcher shop is the kitchen's focal point.* OPPOSITE *Among Nono's prized possessions is a collection of early-20th-century faience from the Aubagne atelier of Louis Sicard, who created beautiful wares in unique sunset colors decorated with landscapes and silhouettes.*

CLOCKWISE FROM TOP Wrought-iron chairs by Jean Feraud in Sarrians seat six comfortably for lunch and dinner chez Nono, often served on the terrace under the trellis; the table is set with a woven tablecloth from Les Toiles du Soleil, octagonal yellow plates from the Poterie Aubagne, antique wine glasses, violet Biot bubble-glass water glasses, and antique Sicard cicada knife rests; two enormous, rib-textured pedestal planters from the La Madeleine potteryworks in Anduze command a corner of the terrace; once farmland and pasture, the terrain extending south from the 19th-century house has been transformed into park-like gardens. OPPOSITE *Sunset imbues Nono's intimate, ocher-pink dining room with an even warmer glow. At night the 19th-century* pâte de verre *(glass-paste) lighting fixture, ornamented with grape clusters, illuminates the room. Elegant Louis XVI dining chairs surround the table, which is usually covered with one of Nono's collection of antique Provençal* piqué *quilts, this one from Marseille.*

the silvery green of the olive trees, to the rich deep green of the cypresses, to the ominous green of the sky just before a big storm?"

Not surprisingly, Nono's house, a spacious 19th-century farmhouse, once a stable, on the outskirts of town, is full of warm, rich color, predominantly shades of red and yellow, giving each room a distinctive glow. A collector at heart, Nono loves regional furniture, paintings, faience, glassware, fabrics, and the unusual *objet,* and the rooms chez Nono reflect her passion. Antique cicadas by Louis Sicard in Aubagne,

RIGHT *The living room's distinctive pharmacy cabinet in walnut, created in the Vaucluse in the early 19th century, is today a handsome bar. On top, an early-20th-century bronze statue of Mistral's heroine, Miréo, keeps company with a terra-cotta bust of the Empress Eugénie.* OPPOSITE *A graceful Napoléon III sofa offers ample seating under an imposing 19th-century still life. A round table dresses up in a vintage silk patchwork quilt.* OVERLEAF, LEFT *In the center of an upstairs hall, a rustic 19th-century pine buffet displays a collection of* tauromachie— *objects relating to bullfighting.* OVERLEAF, RIGHT, Tauromachie *also rules in this guest bedroom, where a 19th-century Italian tole and wrought-iron bed is surrounded by bullfighting paintings, a mounted bull's skull, and an antique sequined toreador's costume.*

terre-melée (mixed-earth) pottery from Gerbino in Vallauris, an 18th-century kidney-shaped pharmacy counter in walnut, a large 1820s floral still life, a Napoleon III sofa, and a 1930s red-enameled bull's head that once decorated a local butcher shop all live happily together in an eclectic, warm, and elegant ambiance that could exist nowhere else but Provence.

☙A FAMILY FARMHOUSE GROWS TO PERFECTION

☙ABOVE *The colors of an early-19th-century* vase d'Anduze, *an orange-tree planter from the famed Boisset atelier, harmonize with the natural hues in Bruno Carles's courtyard.* OPPOSITE *Beneath a sculpted cornice, the sulfate-blue door is framed in blocks of* pierre de Ponotre, *a creamy stone from the region of Sommières.*☙

Bruno Carles's ravishing farmhouse in La Petite Camargue west of Nîmes began life in the 17th century as a humble *mazet*, little more than a hut for sheltering animals and farmworkers from the midday heat, built from ancient Roman stones found scattered in the fields. Over the generations the *mazet* grew, as family and money multiplied, into a modest farmhouse where the family lived alongside small farm animals, later into a cool and airy summer residence, and finally into the solid and sumptuous home it is today for Bruno, one of the region's best-known antiques dealers.

One enters Bruno's domain through a heavy door in a thick stone wall, coming directly into a pebbled courtyard. One's eye is immediately

◄ ABOVE *Across the court-*
yard from the main house
are the former stables,
which Bruno transformed
into a classic orangerie. The
enameled red and yellow
tiles are from Saint Jean de
Fos. The assorted pots come
from both Uzès and Saint
Jean de Fos. BELOW *Behind*
the house, and unseen from
the road, is a gorgeous
surprise—a vast, landscaped
garden with romantic paths
and sheltered niches. OPPO-
SITE *The long, sleek dining*
table with wood-bordered
pierre de Tavel, polished
stone from the region of
Châteauneuf-du-Pape, is a
Bruno Carles design, as are
the rush-seated chairs. The
buffet-à-deux-corps is an
18th-century piece from a
Provençal château, re-
painted by Bruno with
softly gilded, stylized ini-
tials on each door. The
19th-century covered pots
on the table are from Apt.
OVERLEAF *Enhancing the*
kitchen with dynamic color
are tiles from La Bisbal, a
Spanish town of clay arti-
sans. Most of the ceramic
pots on the shelf above
the stove are from Saint
Jean de Fos and Saint-
Quentin-la-Poterie. ◄

caught by gorgeous splashes of blue, a rich and brilliant sulfate-blue conjured by Bruno to trim his home's doors and windows. "The shade is an agricultural blue that I've always found beautiful," he says. "It's the exact color of the copper sulfate sprayed on grapevines—a distinctive, subtly greened blue—to protect them from mildew." The blue paint, which Bruno developed through lengthy trial and error, harmonizes perfectly with the lush, deep green vines that blanket the

house's facade. At the rear of the house, the trim complements the flowers and shrubs in the lavish gardens, planted not only to please the senses, but to attract a wide variety of birds.

Within the house, Bruno has chosen colors that are soft and restful, but still inspired by nature. Interior hues reflect the characteristic tones of the region: a very soft yellow, the lightly ochered color of wheat, and

a soft green-gray, the color, as Bruno describes it, of the underside of an olive leaf. An exacting fellow, Bruno has carefully researched and pursued all the details—colors, decorative elements, and furnishings—in his house. To finish his kitchen, for example, Bruno found the brown and ocher tiles that pleased him in the Spanish town of Bisbal, a few miles south of the French border, where artisans still craft handmade tiles in the 18th-century tradition.

Bruno has filled his home with both the regional antiques he loves and the fine reproductions he has crafted for his shop in Lunel, formerly the home where he grew up. Pieces range from an extremely ornate 18th-century *commode Nîmoise,* (from Nîmes) in the master bedroom to the long stone-topped dining table and 18th-century-style rush-seated chairs, both recent Bruno Carles creations. While most of the house is filled with antiques that have been with him for years, and some of his own creations, an occa-

ABOVE *Formal but welcoming, the living room is warmed by an ornate 18th-century marble fireplace. The 18th century predominates in the room's décor, with a pair of Louis XVI* bibliothèques *flanking the window, and a collection of Louis XVI chairs in a variety of styles. The sofa is contemporary, upholstered in a pattern called "Camargue" from Lauer.* BELOW *A handsomely sculpted white marble sink, hand-printed wallpaper from the Zuber firm in Alsace, and an old family portrait give a tiny guest bathroom presence and personality.* OPPOSITE *The kitchen's ornately sculpted walnut buffet hails from the Languedoc, near Sommières. The still-life painting is by Jean Lamouroux, a contemporary painter working in Sarrians, near Carpentras.*

ABOVE Two pieces of furniture embellish the guest bedroom—an 18th-century walnut armoire from Nîmes, with a floral cut-work base, and an 18th-century walnut commode with floral carving. BELOW The master bedroom boasts an ornately decorated, and rather curiously designed, Empire commode. Above it hangs a portrait of a lady painted around 1760 in Paris. OPPOSITE Seeing this small marble bust again was a pleasant surprise. The statue's head dates from Roman antiquity. Sometime in the late 18th or early 19th century, a torso was sculpted and attached to flesh out the old boy.

sional new acquisition joins the ménage. Like any good dealer, Bruno always has an eye open for the great *trouvaille,* or find. In a small foyer, perched atop an 18th-century marble-topped buffet, is an antique marble bust of an impish, smirking Pan-like figure. "Does it look familiar?" asks Bruno. It did indeed, as it is the same small statue that sits in a niche above the banquette on the

cover of the original *Pierre Deux's French Country.* At the time the cover photograph was taken, the statue resided at the Château de Fontarèches near Uzès. The château and its furnishings were eventually sold and the statue, entering another chapter in its long and perhaps checkered history, made its way to Bruno.

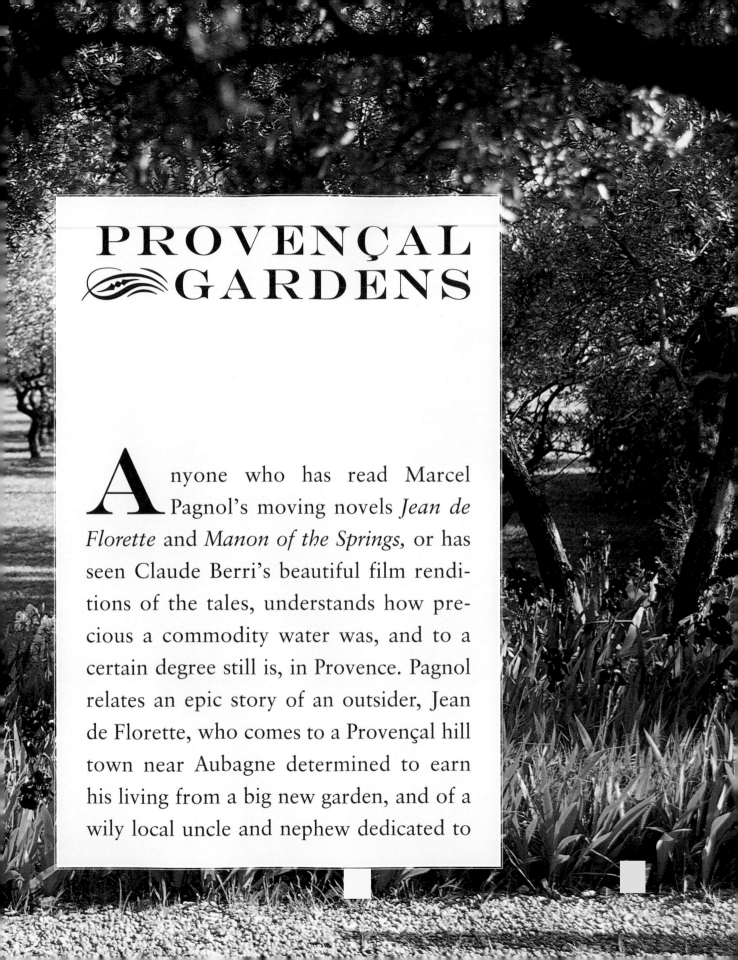

PROVENÇAL GARDENS

Anyone who has read Marcel Pagnol's moving novels *Jean de Florette* and *Manon of the Springs,* or has seen Claude Berri's beautiful film renditions of the tales, understands how precious a commodity water was, and to a certain degree still is, in Provence. Pagnol relates an epic story of an outsider, Jean de Florette, who comes to a Provençal hill town near Aubagne determined to earn his living from a big new garden, and of a wily local uncle and nephew dedicated to

PRECEDING PAGES *In Marco Lillet's simple and lovely Easter garden, purple and white irises bloom in April beneath the olive trees.* ABOVE LEFT *An embroidered pillow casing announcing "I'm in the garden" hangs at the door of the Mas des Beaumes, a bed-and-breakfast in Gordes.* ABOVE RIGHT *Newly planted lavender comes into flower in June at a home in the Luberon.* BELOW *An orchard of cherry trees blooms in the Var in early spring.* OPPOSITE *A small cypress gets cozy with a mass of bridal wreath spirea in an Eygalières garden.*

humiliating him by blocking Florette's spring. Manon, Jean's beautiful daughter, exacts her revenge in the second novel. Provence is an arid region with soils that range from poor and scrubby to rich. Growing almost anything was, and still is, a challenge. Where there was arable land, priorities were always given to plants and trees that provided either food, shade, or shelter from the raging mistral. Floral and other decorative gardens were tremendous luxuries reserved for the rich who lived in grand bastides in Aix, or Marseille, or along the Riviera. What

LEFT *At an estate near Grasse, a long allée guarded by a pair of antique stone lions leads to an 18th-century terra-cotta and stone fountain.* OPPOSITE, CLOCKWISE FROM TOP LEFT *A deserted cobblestone road leads past the daunting limestone walls of the Abbaye Saint-André, a former fortified Benedictine abbey built between the 11th and the 17th centuries in Villeneuve-lès-Avignon; the abbey's glorious gardens are now open to the public, with romantic stone statuary punctuating the paths through the greenery; at the top of a hill above the abbey sits the restored 11th-century Sainte-Césarie chapel; climbing pink roses weave through the wrought-iron trellises in the stone-pillared rose arbor.*

flowers there were, in village homes or on farms, were confined to pots on terraces or windowsills.

Sophisticated irrigation and high-tech hydraulics brought revolutionary change to Provence in the 20th century. Now, at the beginning of the 21st century, gardens flourish everywhere, from farmhouse potagers, kitchen gardens, and small beds of roses behind a village home, to classic terraced gardens—sometimes as grand as parks—stretching out from a *bastide's* or large farmhouse's traditionally

PRECEDING PAGES *The sprawling hill town of Gordes towers over a magnificent landscaped garden in the Luberon. Olive trees, cypresses, and trimmed boxwood dominate the terraced design.* ABOVE *The property of this Luberon estate, a cluster of small, interconnected farmhouses, was once a self-contained hamlet surrounded by farmland.* BELOW *Ancient drystone walls typical of the area have been preserved on the property.* OPPOSITE, CLOCKWISE FROM TOP LEFT *A refreshing pool reserved for frogs and their lily pads provides cool respite on a summer day under the blazing Provençal sun; the parklike gardens are primarily green and sculptural, with visual interest sparked by shapes, textures, and tonalities of green; reinforced drystone walls called* restanques *separate one level of garden from another; stretching beyond an antique well in the lower gardens, vineyards and olive groves stretch to the horizon.*

southern-facing facade. There are specialized gardens, like Marco Lillet's lovely Easter garden in Eygalières, blooming with gorgeous blue, purple, and white irises under the olive trees; the lush organic garden at the Mas de la Chassagnette in the Camargue, surveyed by a dapper scarecrow named Monsieur Jean; and the heavenly terraced gardens of the Abbaye de Saint-André in Villeneuve-lès-Avignon, filled with irises, olive trees, roses, wisteria, oleanders, lovely walking paths, and an 11th-century chapel. Then there are the sensuous, sculptural, and predominantly green gardens designed by Michel Semini, an influential landscape architect in the Luberon, including his own tiny and captivating garden hidden behind the high walls of his village home; an unusual garden near Saint-Rémy with a fully decorated gypsy wagon as its focal point; and, perhaps the ultimate luxury in this parched landscape, lush, green lawns.

Terraced gardens, a landscape design particularly well-suited to the local terrain, were fashionable in Provence in the early decades of the 1900s, but most eventually went to seed because the châteaux or villas they adjoined were rented out or had been abandoned by the early 1940s. Two World Wars took their toll on the inhabitants and their

LEFT *Stone-paved paths lead to the terrace of a house near Grasse, where large urns of potted flowers dot the terrace.* RIGHT *Looking at the same house from a different angle, a row of potted boxwood demarcate the edge of a garden.* OPPOSITE *A variety of stone or terra-cotta pots are the planters of choice in stylish Provençal gardens; most sought after are antique Anduze pots, bottom right.* OVERLEAF *An estate in Grasse offers one of the best examples in the entire region of a beautiful, traditional terraced garden, with the* restanques *(rustic stone walls) reinforcing each level.*

*LEFT Two towering
cypress trees stand like sentinels next to a grand
bastide in the Luberon.
RIGHT Just outside the
kitchen, a cool and shady
terrace is the ideal spot
for an alfresco dinner.
OPPOSITE Over eight years,
this bastide's meticulously
landscaped gardens grew
larger and more defined,
eventually covering many
acres of terraced plantings.
A collaboration between
the owners and landscape
architect Michel Semini,
the design theme was pri-
marily a "green garden,"
very sculptural and Medi-
terranean, characterized by
densely massed greenery, a
play of light and shade, and
clusters of sensuous, precisely trimmed boxwood
spheres. The Adirondack-
style teak table and
chairs are from Tectona.
OVERLEAF To give the
owner of the bastide a
place to store her garden
tools and work with cut
flowers, Michel Semini
designed this unique,
vintage-looking cabinet and
étagère of tole and wrought
iron in the house's light-
filled orangerie.*

finances. In recent years, with ample supplies of time, money, and water, terraced gardens have been reborn. Their designs were inspired originally by both the more formal and structured *jardin à la française,* conceived by the seminal 17th-century landscape architect André LeNôtre, and the romantic Italianate garden with its terraced design and its stone muses.

The landscaping of a traditional terraced property begins not with the gardens themselves, but with the entry to the property: a long *allée* of plane trees flanking the drive up to the house. Then attention was focused on the terrace, which extends from the southern, and almost always front, facade of the house. For any Provençal home, except village houses fronting the street, a terrace is essential, serving as an outdoor living room for sunny days that also links the interior and the exterior of the property. De rigueur for the terrace are tall shade trees, such as plane trees, lindens, or chestnuts, which shelter the terrace with their broad, leafy canopies. The trees are traditionally planted in a row of three, a mystical number in Provence representing the Trinity; cypresses, particularly at the entrance to a property, are also planted in

a cluster of three. Another integral component of the terrace is the trellis over the doorway, either a simple tangle of lush vines shading the entrance like a small awning, or a large pergola or arbor that shades an expanse of the terrace for dining. (Some purists don't believe a pergola or arbor is in harmony with classic Provençal architecture, but those who enjoy the structure's beauty and cool shade heartily disagree.) Many types of vines are used for the Provençal trellis, among them wisteria, honeysuckle, grapes, trumpet vines, Virginia creeper, and jasmine. Completing the classic terrace is a worn stone bench placed flush with the wall of the house just outside the front door, and an old stone well just off to the side.

The embankment separating one level of garden from the next is usually a reinforced drystone wall called a *restanque*; a short flight of steps often bisects the wall, giving access to the next terrace. Down the steps to the second terraced level are small flower gardens, perhaps a matching pair, sometimes framed by boxwood parterres. Among the flowers blooming within might be roses, marguerites, geraniums, lavender certainly, irises, lilies, white syringas, verbena, and convolvulus. Lilacs may bloom nearby along with mimosa and bougainvillea, if the garden is in

LEFT The bassin of a Luberon bastide reflects the silhouetted iron figures of two women by sculptor Laurence Ambrose; in the distance are the ruins of the Marquis de Sade's 42-room château in Lacoste. RIGHT *On the same property, a gently arched pergola bordered by a wrought-iron gate shades a small terrace off the kitchen.* OPPOSITE, CLOCKWISE FROM TOP LEFT *A low wooden door leads into landscape architect Michel Semini's private walled garden; shallow stone steps wind down to a stone terrace, shaded by palms, which borders a swimming pool; paved with ancient stones, the garden has little earth for planting, so Michel makes this hidden garden lush and verdant with dozens of potted flowers and shrubs.*

THIS PAGE AND OPPOSITE
*Part of a vast property in
the Camargue, the Mas de
la Chassagnette is both a
restaurant and a wonderful
organic vegetable garden.
It covers almost 2,000
square feet in the midst of
130 acres of farmland that
produce rice, lentils, hard-
wheat, and soy. Surround-
ing a central fountain,
above right, a large array of
aromatic herbs, vegetables,
fruits, and flowers fills the
garden, among them cab-
bages, zucchini, and
arugula. The garden grows
under the watchful eye of
the scarecrow, Monsieur
Jean, above left.*

CLOCKWISE FROM TOP LEFT *The highlight of an unusual garden near Saint-Rémy is a vintage* roulotte *(gypsy wagon), restored to be whimsical guest quarters, and furnished—by the owner, a Paris fashion designer—with colorful flea-market kitsch, to be true to type; a stylized copper armillary sphere poised on an old stone pedestal commands its own garden niche; the gypsy wagon opens onto a shady olive grove; the olive trees give the house and the gypsy wagon a modicum of mutual privacy.* OPPOSITE *Within view of the gypsy wagon, a lush grape arbor shades a long farm table covered with a vintage quilt and surrounded by a set of early-20th-century rattan chairs.*

the southernmost part of Provence. Also on the second level of the terraced garden are one or two indispensable fig trees and a couple of lovely almond trees, the very first harbingers of spring, with their fragrant white or pink blossoms opening in late February, long before spring itself arrives.

On the third terraced level, again down several stone steps, would be a much larger swath of land planted with a small orchard: neat rows of olive, cherry, or apricot trees, and to one side a substantial *potager* garden. The classic kitchen garden contains both herbs and vegetables, and occasionally berries and melons. Tomatoes, French beans, tiny purple artichokes, squashes, lettuces, garlic, scallions, basil, oregano, dill, parsley, sage, rosemary, and thyme flourish from late spring to late summer. To complete the classically landscaped property would be a small vineyard at the side or back of the house, and a wall of tall cypresses planted like a soaring hedge to protect the house and garden from the powerful mistral blowing from the north. Most Provençal gardens today, even the fashionable and predominantly green gardens featuring sculpted forms of santolina, sage, boxwood, yews, and lavender, boast elements of the classic terraced garden.

Despite the growing number of large and lavish gardens blooming throughout Provence, the plethora of aromatic *potagers,* and even the countless small rock gardens or hedge-bordered flower gardens, the most ubiquitous and representative garden for me remains the little potted garden. Bursts of startling color punctuate windowsills, doorways, terraces, outdoor stairways, backyard paths, poolside embankments, and no-longer-functioning wells. Contained in a motley collection of clustered ceramic pots—glazed and unglazed, large and small, perfect and chipped—these casually assembled floral displays can be lovingly cared for with little effort and modest amounts of water. Wherever your travels in the region may take you, through city streets, down village *ruelles,* or along country paths, splashes and patches of vivid hues—a wine barrel holding a burst of pink hydrangeas, cascades of crimson geraniums overflowing their sun-bleached terra-cotta pots—will catch your eye, coloring forever your memory of Provence.

CLOCKWISE FROM TOP LEFT *A trellis of climbing roses shades the entrance of an 18th-century farmhouse in Goult; a lush canopy of old wisteria shelters a doorway at a* bastide *near Bonnieux; grapevines arch over a stairway near Les Baux; on a clear December day, a thick arc of pyracantha cloaks the entrance to the Mas des Graviers, a bed-and-breakfast in Pourrières, near Aix-en-Provence.* OVERLEAF, LEFT *Ripe apricots beckon from an orchard at the foot of Les Baux de Provence.* OVERLEAF, RIGHT, *Lunch is served at the Mas de la Barjolle in Fontvieille.*

DIRECTORY

A Guide to French Country Sources in Provence

In the course of researching this book, seeking out the best of all things authentically Provençal, we visited dozens of regional shops, ateliers, and markets. In this directory we offer an overview of sources for furniture, fabrics, faience, tiles, architectural salvage, and a broad range of decorative accessories. We also include some of our favorite hotels and bed-and-breakfast inns where you can stay in style during your visit to Provence. The addresses dot the map of the region, and perhaps a dozen of them linked together would comprise an intriguing itinerary. Provence is a cornucopia of regional treasures; here we present a pocket guide of where to find them. When calling France from abroad, first dial 33, then drop the first 0.

ANTIQUE ARCHITECTURAL ELEMENTS

Restored and unrestored architectural elements are in high demand not only in Provence but throughout France. Nothing gives charm and character to a house like antique stonework, period tiles, or a vintage mantelpiece.

JEAN CHABAUD, LES MATÉRIAUX ANCIENS
21, route de Gargas
84400 Apt
04-90-74-07-61
Antique carved stone mantelpieces, garden statues, canal tiles, street signs, stone fountains, and much more.

Jean Chabaud, Les Matériaux Anciens

ALAIN GAUTHEY
Route de Draguignan
83690 Salernes
04-94-70-60-77
A skilled stonecutter who restores or copies period mantelpieces.

LES MILLES ET UNE PORTES
Place Emile Zola
83570 Carcès
04-94-04-50-27
Antique doors of all sorts, perhaps even 1,001, as well as vintage paneling, antique furniture, and bibelots.

PORTES ANCIENNES/ANTIQUE DOORS
Route d'Avignon
13210 Saint-Rémy-de-Provence
04-90-92-13-13
A wide selection of, not surprisingly, antique doors.

ANTIQUES

This listing of dealers barely scratches the surface of the French antiques world in Provence, but they are dealers we know and recommend. The very best, most comprehensive, and most up-to-date listing of French antiques dealers—covering all regions of France—is the *Guide Emer,* published yearly and widely available in most bookstores throughout France. The *Guide* lists dealers by region and by specialty, including dealers in antique tile, stonework, wrought iron, lace, and paneling, as well as furniture, and no serious collector would make a buying trip in France without it.

ANTIQUITÉS MAURIN
4, rue de Grille
13200 Arles
04-90-96-51-57
www.antiquites-maurin.com

JEAN-JACQUES BOURGEOIS
(VINCENT MIT L'ÂNE)
5, avenue des Quatre-Otages
84800 L'Isle-sur-la-Sorgue
04-90-20-30-63-15
Antiques and reproductions.

BRUNO CARLES
209–235, avenue de Lattre-de-Tassigny
34400 Lunel
04-67-71-36-10
www.brunocarles.fr
Antiques and reproductions.

F. DERVIEUX
5, rue Vernon
13200 Arles
04-90-96-02-39
Antiques and reproductions.

GÉRARD GUERRE
1, plan de Lunel
84000 Avignon
04-90-86-42-67

NATHALIE LÉGIER
Avenue des Quatre-Otages
84000 L'Isle-sur-la-Sorgue
04-90-38-03-30

CATHERINE LIGEARD
Rue de la République
84220 Goult
06-72-71-08-27

LE MAS DE CUREBOURG (HÉLÈNE
DEGRUGILLIER-DAMPEINE)
Route d'Apt
84800 L'Isle-sur-la-Sorgue
04-90-20-30-06

MONLEAU
44, rue Nationale
30300 Vallabrègues
04-66-59-20-17
*Period reproduction chairs and
banquettes.*

ROBERT REYRE
7, rue Granet
13100 Aix-en-Provence
04-42-23-31-44

Bruno Carles

BEADED CURTAINS

The number of artisans creating handmade, wood-beaded curtains in France has dwindled to a handful. Marie-Claude Brochet, who works in her atelier just south of Avignon exclusively with sleek boxwood beads, is one of the best. Her curtains adorn both doors and windows. She has a variety of styles available and all are made to order.

Marie-Claude Brochet ❧

Below are a handful of top decorators whose work distinguishes some of the finest and most charming homes throughout Provence. Most speak English.

PATRICE ARNOUD
Mas Piédache
84580 Oppède-le-Vieux
04-90-76-99-08

PHILIPPE ECKERT
Mas de la Dame
Chemin St. Gabriel
13160 La Crau de Chateaurenard
04-32-62-10-45

DAN KIENER
14, rue Rambuteau
75003 Paris
01-42-74-79-70

BRUNO LAFOURCADE
Bureau d'Etudes Bruno Lafourcade
10, boulevard Mirabeau
Saint-Rémy-de-Provence
04-90-92-19-14

MARIE-CLAUDE BROCHET
1043, avenue des Vertes-Rives
84140 Montfavet
04-90-23-58-37

MARIE-JOSÉ POMMEREAU
Mortemard & Pommereau
14, rue Clément Marot
75008 Paris
01-47-23-45-96

CANDLES ❧
Almost one hundred years old, the famous *ciergerie* (candleworks) in Graveson produces handcrafted, dripless beeswax and paraffin tapers, votives, and novelty candles for churches, hotels, and the home.

CIERGERIE DES PRÉMONTRÉS
2, avenue François Atget
Graveson
04-90-95-71-14

ESTELLE RÉALE
Villa Estelle
5, montée de la Bourgade
86800 Hauts-de-Cagnes
04-92-02-89-83

AILEEN STEINBACH
Camille-en-Provence
84220 Lumières
Goult
04-90-72-35-45
www.camille-en-provence.com

FABRICS

The floral-sprigged and paisley cottons in brilliant colors still saturate the region, but new fabrics, motifs, and colorations—toiles, softly hued linens, and hand-embroidered textiles—have recently attracted trendsetters and decorators in Provence. There are also shops that have created curtains, aprons, pillows, and other home accessories from bits of antique fabrics, and shops offering well-styled clothes with a regional flavor, to carry *le style provençal* into your wardrobe.

TRADITIONAL FABRIC HOUSES

LES INDIENNES DE NÎMES (TISSUS LE MISTRAL)
2, boulevard des Arènes
30000 Nîmes
(and boutiques in many towns, such as Saint-Rémy, Aix, Moustiers, and Nice)
04-66-83-49-16
www.indiennes-de-nimes.fr

LES OLIVADES
Chemin des Indienneurs
13103 Saint-Etienne-du-Grès
(and boutiques throughout France)
04-90-49-19-19
www.les-olivades.com

SOULEIADO
39, rue Proudhon
13150 Tarascon
(and boutiques throughout France)
04-90-91-50-11
www.souleiadousa.com and
www.souleiado.fr

VALDRÔME
5 bis, rue Louis Barthou
82400 Valence
04-75-43-35-05
www.valdrome.com

SPECIALTY FABRIC BOUTIQUES

ATELIER DU PRESBYTÈRE
10, rue du Presbytère
30300 Vallabrègues
04-66-59-37-37
Unique aprons, pillows, curtains, tableclothes, and bibs from antique textiles by Françoise Méchin-Pellet; also, contemporary ready-to-wear clothing from lush, modern textiles.

CAMILLE
5, boulevard Georges-Clémenceau
13200 Arles
04-90-96-04-94
The *place* for Provençal cowboy gear: *brightly printed shirts, black velour jackets, snug gray riding britches, bolos, and more.*

CAMILLE EN PROVENCE
Lumières
84200 Goult
04-90-72-35-45
www.camille-en-provence.com
Elegant tablecloths, table runners, pillows, curtains in lavish fabrications by Aline Steinbach; also, rare, high-end 15th- to 18th-century antiques in her husband's downstairs antiques shop.

Les Olivades

Vernin, Carreaux D'Apt

DÉCO SUD
17 avenue Gabriel Péri
83740 La Cadière d'Azur
04-90-98-21-77
*From decorator Marie-Anne Echegu,
beautiful, lined tablecloths, hand-
stitched from vintage fabrics, as well
as aprons, pillows, and handsome
regional tableware.*

LA MAISON BIEHN
7, rue des Quatre-Otages
84800 L'Isle-sur-la-Sorgue
04-90-20-89-04
*A wonderful collection of antique
Provençal fabrics, antique quilts, and
rustic contemporary linens.*

EDITH MÉZARD
Château de L'Ange
84200 Lumières
04-90-72-36-41
Exquisite hand-embroidered table linens.

LE RIDEAU DE PARIS
32, rue de Bac
75007 Paris
01-42-61-18-56
*Florence Maeght produces fine reproduc-
tions for her collections of 18th- and
19th-century textiles and quilts, tablecloths, place mats, handbags, and more.*

FAIENCE, POTTERY, AND TILES

The following firms produce all
kinds of pottery, from great terra-
cotta urns to marbled-clay dinnerware to whimsically patterned plates
and platters. Also listed are producers of glazed and unglazed tiles for
interior and exterior uses.

ATELIER ALAIN VAGH
Route d'Entrecasteaux
83630 Salernes
04-94-70-61-85
*One of the best artisans in this famous
village of tile makers, with plain and
patterned tiles in traditional and contemporary designs.*

ATELIER SOLEIL
Chemin Marcel-Provence and Chemin
Quinson
04360 Moustiers-Sainte-Marie
04-92-74-63-05
*Traditional Moustiers faience, white
glaze over red clay, and polychrome
décors of flowers, Revolutionary motifs,
and grotesques.*

CAROCIM
Quartier Beaufort
CD 14
13540 Puyricard
04-42-92-20-39
*Beautifully hued, batch-dyed cement
tiles, some matte finish; 19th-century
vintage, new and Souleiado patterns.*

FAIENCE D'APT: JEAN FAUCON
(Atelier Bernard)
12, avenue de la Libération
84400 Apt
04-90-74-15-31
*Exquisite and unique marbled-clay
faience, produced by the family of the
late faiencier Jean Faucon.*

VÉRONIQUE PICHON
19 bis, avenue de la Gare
30700 Uzès
Continuing the long tradition of Pichon faience in elegant, often art-deco or turn-of-the-century designs.

ANTONY PITOT
Quartier de Ponty
Route Nationale 100
84220 Goult
04-90-72-22-79
Fine yellow and green faience in the 18th-century Apt tradition.

POTERIE DE HAUTE PROVENCE
Route de Nyons
26220 Dieulefit
04-75-46-42-10
Rustic glazed pots and dinnerware from a traditional and picturesque pottery village.

POTERIE RAVEL
Avenue des Goums
13400 Aubagne
04-42-18-79-79
A venerable family company producing large unglazed terra-cotta planters as well as glazed yellow and green dinnerware for more than 100 years.

VERNIN, CARREAUX D'APT
Route Nationale 100 (Pont Julien)
84480 Bonnieux
04-90-04-63-04
www.carreaux-d-apt.com
Dazzling handmade, hand-painted glazed tiles in 165 gorgeous colors; custom patterns of your choice to order.

GARDEN DESIGNERS ☞

Two of the most prolific and respected garden designers in the Luberon and Bouches-du-Rhône regions are Michel Semini, whose distinctive monochromatic "green" gardens appear in the pages of this

☞ *Jean-Claude Guigne, harvest ladder*

book, and Dominique Lafourcade, whose work, on the garden of Jean-André and Geneviève Charial, also graces these pages.

DOMINIQUE LAFOURCADE
10, boulevard Mirabeau
13210 Saint-Rémy-de-Provence
04-90-92-10-14

MICHEL SEMINI
Rue Saint-Frusquain
84220 Goult
04-90-72-38-50

Hotel La Mirande

GLASSWARE

Biot is the spot for the distinctive, rustic bubble-glass that coordinates so beautifully with the regional country-style tableware and linens. Glasses, vases, ice buckets, hurricane lamps, and more in clear and very pale blue, green, and violet hues. The Verrerie ships all over the world.

VERRERIE DE BIOT
5, Chemin des Combes
06410 Biot
04-93-65-03-00

HOTELS AND B&B'S

There are many stylish hotels and bed-and-breakfasts in Provence that will enhance your visit to the region with the warmth of their welcome. The following hostelries offer a wide variety of accommodations, settings, and décor, from restored antique properties in the old quarters of cities such as Saint-Rémy, Arles, and Avignon, to a hillside farmhouse roost nestled in the countryside of the Alpes-de-Hautes-Provence, to a handsome ranch house deep in the Camargue. All are rich in the flavors of Provence and are decorated with authentic elements and ample good taste. Remember, when calling any of these places from the United States, dial 011-33, then drop the first "0" of the telephone number. When calling from France, dial the number as written.

HOTELS

LA BASTIDE DE MARIE
Route de Bonnieux
Quartier de la Verrerie
84360 Ménerbes
04-90-72-30-20
www.c-h-m.com

LA BASTIDE DE MOUSTIERS
Chemin de Quinson
84360 Moustiers-Sainte-Marie
04-92-70-47-47
www.chateauxhotels.com/moustiers

LE CAGNARD
Rue Sous Barri
06800 Hauts-de-Cagnes
04-93-20-73-21
www.le-cagnard.com

CHÂTEAU DE ROCHEGUDE
26790 Rochegude (Drôme)
04-75-97-21-10
www.chateaurochegude.com

GRAND HOTEL NORD-PINUS
Place du Forum
13200 Arles
04-90-93-44-44
www.nord-pinus.com

HOSTELLERIE DE L'ABBAYE
DE LA CELLE
Place du Général de Gaulle
83170 La Celle (near Brignoles)
04-98-06-14-14
www.abbaye-celle.com

HOSTELLERIE BÉRARD
83740 La Cadière-d'Azur
04-94-90-11-43
www.hotel-berard.com

HOTEL DU CASTELLET
3001, Routes des Hauts de Camp
83330 Le Beausset
04-94-98-37-77
www.hotelducastellet.com

HOTEL SAINT PAUL
86, rue Grande
06570 Saint-Paul-de-Vence
04-93-32-65-25
www.lesaintpaul.com

LE MAS CANDILLE
Boulevard Clément-Rebuffel
06250 Mougins
04-92-28-43-43
www.lemascandille.com

LE MAS DE PEINT
13200 Le Sambuc (Arles)
04-92-97-20-62
www.chateauxhotels.com/maspeint

MICHEL CHABRAN
29, avenue du 45ème Parallèle
26600 Pont-de-L'Isère (Drôme)
04-75-84-60-09
www.chateauxhotels.com/chabran

LA MIRANDE
4, Place L'Amirande
84800 Avignon
04-90-85-93-93
www.la-mirande.fr

LES MUSCADINS
18, boulevard Georges Courteline
06250 Mougins
04-92-28-28-28
www.chateauxhotels.com/muscadins

OUSTAU DE BAUMANIÈRE
13520 Les-Baux-de-Provence
04-90-54-40-46
www.oustaudebaumaniere.com or
www.relaischateaux.com/oustau

VILLA GALLICI
Avenue de la Violette
13100 Aix-en-Provence
04-42-23-29-23
www.relaischateaux.com/gallici

BED-AND-BREAKFASTS

LE CLOS DES SAUMANES
519, chemin de la Garrigue
84470 Châteauneuf-de-Gadagne
(near Avignon)
04-90-08-22-19
E-mail: closaumane@aol.com

LA MAISON DES SOURCES
Chemin des Fraisses
84360 Lauris (near Lourmarin)
04-90-08-22-19
www.maison-des-sources.com

LA MAISON DU VILLAGE
10, rue du 8 Mai
13210 Saint-Rémy-de-Provence
04-32-60-68-20
www.lamaisonduvillage.com

LE MAS DE LA BEAUME
84220 Gordes Village
04-90-72-02-96
www.la.beaume.com

➣ En route to Maussane

LE MAS DES FONTAINES
Route du Destet
13520 Maussane-les-Alpilles
04-90-54-22-81
E-mail: mas.des.fontaines@online.fr

LE MAS DES GRAVIERS
Route du Rians
Chemin Cézanne
83910 Pourrières
04-94-78-40-38

LA PAULINE
"Les Pinchinats"
Chemin de la Fontaine des Tuiles
13100 Aix-en-Provence
04-42-17-02-60
www.la-pauline.com

VILLA ESTELLE
5, Montée de la Bourgade
06800 Hauts-de-Cagnes
04-92-02-89-83
www.villa-estelle.com

MUSEUMS AND HISTORIC CHÂTEAUX

Visiting several of the fascinating museums that dot Provence would enrich any vacation in the region.

Musée Fragonard

Museums appeal to a wide variety of special interests, including art, faience, fabrics, furniture, perfume, and even the nitty-gritty of paint.

ANCIENNE USINE
MATHIEU/CONSERVATOIRE DES
OCRES ET PIGMENTS APPLIQUÉS
(APPLIED OCHER AND PIGMENTS
REPOSITORY)
Route d'Apt, D.104
84200 Roussillon
04-90-05-66-69
A former ocher mill exists today as an unusual museum within the old quarries. It is also the setting for a wide range of art courses focusing on the use of color and includes a color library.

ATELIER PAUL CÉZANNE
9, avenue Paul Cézanne
13100 Aix-en-Provence
04-42-21-06-53
Cézanne's atelier in the hills above Aix.

CHÂTEAU D'ANSOUIS
84240 Ansouis (near Lourmarin)
04-90-09-82-70
The residence of the Duke and Duchess de Sabran, which is part of this historic and elegant château, is open for public visits and is the site of many open-air concerts in the summer months. Don't miss the château's large, old-fashioned Provençal kitchen.

CHÂTEAU DE BARBENTANE
13570 Barbentane (near Saint-Rémy)
04-90-95-51-07
A lavish late-17th-century château that reveals the strong influence of Italy on the wealthy and aristocratic of the era.

FRÉDÉRIC MISTRAL MUSEUM
11, avenue Lamartine
13910 Maillane
04-90-95-74-06
The former home, preserved intact, of the great Provençal poet and winner of the Nobel Prize for Literature, Frédéric Mistral (1830–1914).

MUSÉE DES ARTS ET TRADITIONS
POPULAIRES DU CHÂTEAU
GOMBERT
5, places des Héros
13013 Marseille
04-91-68-14-38
*A historic château with a vast collection
of regional costumes and furniture.*

MUSÉE CHARLES-
DEMÉRY/SOULEIADO
39, rue Proudhon
13150 Tarascon
04-90-91-08-80
*A charming Provençal art de vivre
museum, featuring fabrics, faience, and
furniture, sheltered within the walled
confines of Souleiado's mansion headquarters.*

MUSÉE DE LA FAÏENCE/CHÂTEAU
PASTRÉ
155, avenue de Nontredon
13008 Marseilles
04-91-72-43-47
*A wonderful collection of antique
faience in a beautiful château–park
setting.*

MUSÉE FRAGONARD
20, boulevard Fragonard
06130 Grasse
04-93-36-44-65
*A fascinating museum of perfume, with
displays of antique costumes and jewelry from the grand collection of the
Costa family.*

MUSÉE MASSÉNA
65, rue de France
06000 Nice
04-93-88-11-34
Provençal furniture and faience.

MUSÉE DE LA POTERIE
Rue Sicard
06220 Vallauris
04-93-64-66-51
*A museum of antique faience and
pottery in one of France's most famous
pottery towns.*

Savonnerie Marius Fabre

MUSÉON ARLATEN
29, rue de la République
13200 Arles
04-90-93-58-11
*An intriguing museum of Provençal life,
arts, and craft.*

OLIVE-OIL
SOAPS

Big square blocks of olive-oil soap
have been made in Provence for
more than one hundred years. The
pale greenish soap cubes are practical as well as rustically beautiful.
One of the most renowned companies still producing artisanal soap
the old-fashioned way is Marius
Fabre. There is a small soap museum
on site.

SAVONNERIE MARIUS FABRE
148, avenue Paul-Bourret
13300 Salon-de-Provence
04-90-53-24-77

PROVENÇAL HARVEST LADDERS ⤫

The shop of Jean-Claude Guigne is one of the last places in Provence to produce the picturesque three-point wooden harvest ladder. This unique ladder was once ubiquitous in cherry and apricot orchards, and was widely used in olive groves over the past hundred years, but, sadly, it is viewed as an anachronism today and is rapidly disappearing.

JEAN-CLAUDE GUIGNE
4, place Emile-Combes
84400 Tarascon
04-90-91-04-99

The Mediterranean, viewed from the hills above Grasse ⤫

SANTON MAKERS ⤫

The following *santonniers* produce beguiling *santons* in a broad range of sizes, colors, and styles, from miniature hand-molded, hand-painted figures in terra-cotta, to large, doll-size creations with hand-sculpted heads and articulated bodies dressed in hand-stitched Provençal costumes.

ATELIERS CARBONEL
47, rue Neuve-Sainte-Catherine
13007 Marseille
www.santonsmarcelcarbonel.com
04-91-54-26-58

CASTELIN-PEIRANO
17, avenue Gabriel Péri
13400 Aubagne
04-42-03-19-11

MAMIE MARTIN
10, rue Hôpital-Vieux
83630 Aups
04-94-70-10-78

SANTONS FOUQUES
65 Cours Gambetta
13100 Aix-en-Provence
04-42-26-33-38

TRADITIONAL PROVENÇAL HOUSE PAINTS ⤫

Among the few remaining companies that still produce authentic tinted lime washes colored with natural local pigments extracted from the nearby Gargas quarries is the Société des Ocres de France.

SOCIÉTÉ DES OCRES DE FRANCE
Impasse des Ocriers
84400 Apt
04-90-74-63-82

VACATION RENTALS

There are many ways to find a lovely short-term rental in Provence. In my experience, the best means are either a local real-estate agent or the websites of regional organizations or tourist bureaus. You will generally pay about half of what you would if you arrange your rental through a U.S.-based agency. Below are just a handful of suggestions. The Internet, particularly a search engine such as Google, will provide many more.

LUBÉRON INVESTISSEMENTS
La Combe
84220 Gordes
04-90-72-07-55
www.lubinvest.com
Agent extraordinaire and man-about-Provence Vincent Boeuf and his large team offer high-quality, mostly luxe rentals throughout the Luberon, as well as in Aix-en-Provence, Fontvieille, Lourmarin, Manosque, Saint-Saturnin-d'Apt, and other locations. The agency is also a renowned real-estate firm selling many of the region's most sought-after properties. His clientele spans the globe from Hong Kong and Brunei to Hollywood and Paris.

LUBERON NEWS MAGAZINE
www.luberon-news.com
This online site, with information in both French and English, is a font of information on the Luberon region. It features vacation rentals, real-estate agents, bed-and-breakfasts, festivals, markets, museums, sports activities, and much more. Individuals list their properties for rent, without agents involved, so the prices are excellent, although it's a leap of faith to rent one sight unseen. But there are good properties at good values among the listings. Photos or websites, and lengthy descriptions, are almost always available.

Jean Feraud, Ferronnier

UN MAS EN PROVENCE
Immobilier Estate Agents
84220 Hameau de Coustellet (Gordes)
04-90-76-75-00
E-mail: masprov@aol.com
A fine small agency handling properties primarily in the Lubéron.

WROUGHT IRON

Several top artisans produce fine hand-worked wrought-iron stair rails, mirrors, chandeliers, garden furniture, gates, and more.

GÉRARD AUDE,
FERRONNERIE D'ART
84220 Saint-Pantaléon (Gordes)
04-90-72-22-67

JEAN FERAUD, FERRONNIER
Boulevard Roumanille
84260 Sarrians
04-90-65-41-37

INDEX